HOME & HERITAGE

MEMBER RECIPES

Cooking Club of America®

Minnetonka, Minnesota

HOME & HERITAGE
MEMBER RECIPES

Tom Carpenter
Creative Director

Heather Koshiol
Managing Editor

Jennifer Weaverling
Senior Book Development Coordinator

Greg Schwieters
Book Design

Gina Germ
Book Production

Laura Holle
Senior Book Development Assistant

Lisa Golden Schroeder
Recipe Selection

Bill Lindner
Commissioned Photography

Abby Wyckoff
Food Stylist

Susan Telleen
Assistant Food Stylist

Rhonda Watkins
Prop Stylist

Special Thanks To: Terry Casey, Janice Cauley, Pat Durkin, Elizabeth Gunderson, Jason Lund, Ruth Petran and Jon Storm.

On Cover: Spiced Cranberry Pear Cobbler, page 115
On Page 1: Apple-Stuffed Pork Loin, page 39

4 5 6 7 8 / 11 10 09 08 07
ISBN 10: 1-58159-183-7
ISBN 13: 978-1-58159-183-5
©2003 Cooking Club of America

Cooking Club of America
12301 Whitewater Drive
Minnetonka, MN 55343
www.cookingclub.com

Overnight Pecan Rolls
Page 14

Asparagus with Citrus Vinaigrette, Page 27

Chicken Cacciatore
Page 44

Squash Apple Bake
Page 56

Chicken & Dumplings
Page 75

CONTENTS

Greek New Year's Bread
Page 88

Cranberry Cheese Strudel
Page 105

Classic Lemon Tart
Page 120

Raisin Lebkuchen
Page 138

Garden Relish
Page 153

WELCOME

Welcome to one of the finest cookbooks you'll ever hold.

What makes these pages so special? The generosity of the Cooking Club of America Members who so freely and eagerly shared their time-honored, heirloom and traditional recipes for all of us to enjoy.

These dishes, meals, desserts and treats are woven into the fabric of your fellow members' home life — the culinary creations they turn to when a celebration of some type is planned, company is coming or the family just needs a good meal they love, to keep energized and going.

These foods also represent the heritage of your fellow members. Many of these recipes have been handed down from generation to generation, and between family members and friends as well; they truly are a part of the legacy of each and every family represented.

Those are the gifts you'll find upon these pages. We sincerely hope you appreciate the generosity of Cooking Club of America Members who shared a part of their **Home & Heritage** to help create this book.

You're sure to find some recipes that will become part of your life as well.

BREAKFASTS & BRUNCHES

CHILE CHEESE PUFF

MARILYN GRAESSER
CHICO, CALIFORNIA

Serve this great breakfast casserole with fresh fruit and coffee cake.

10　eggs, beaten
½　cup all-purpose flour
1　teaspoon salt
2　cups small-curd cottage cheese
½　cup butter, melted
1　lb. jack cheese, shredded
1　(7-oz.) can green chiles

❶ Heat oven to 375°F. Spray 3-quart glass casserole with nonstick cooking spray.

❷ In large bowl, combine eggs, flour, salt, cottage cheese, butter and jack cheese; blend well. Stir in chiles. Pour mixture into casserole. Bake 35 minutes or until knife inserted near center comes out clean.

6 servings.

HASH BROWN QUICHE

BETTY BOSWELL
WACO, TEXAS

I like to take this dish to my church brunches. It's always a favorite.

3　cups frozen, loose-pack, shredded hash browns, thawed
⅓　cup butter, melted
1　cup chopped cooked ham
1　cup (4 oz.) shredded cheddar cheese
¼　cup diced green bell pepper
2　eggs
½　cup milk
½　teaspoon salt
¼　teaspoon freshly ground pepper

❶ Heat oven to 425°F. Press hash browns between paper towels to remove excess moisture. Press hash browns into bottom and up sides of 9-inch pie plate; drizzle with butter. Bake 25 minutes.

❷ In medium bowl, combine ham, cheddar and bell pepper; mix well. Spoon mixture into crust. In small bowl, beat eggs, milk, salt and pepper; mix well. Pour over ham mixture. Reduce oven temperature to 325°F. Bake 25 to 30 minutes or until knife inserted near center comes out clean. Let stand 10 minutes before serving.

6 servings.

SMOKED SALMON CHEESECAKE

ANITA COYNE
BONITA SPRINGS, FLORIDA

Here's one of our family's favorite Christmas treats.

⅓　cup dry bread crumbs
¼　cup plus 2 tablespoons freshly grated Parmesan cheese
2　teaspoons butter
⅓　cup chopped onion
⅓　cup chopped green onions, including tops
4　(8-oz.) pkg. cream cheese, at room temperature
4　eggs
½　cup heavy cream
½　lb. unsalted smoked salmon, coarsely chopped
½　teaspoon salt
¼　teaspoon freshly ground pepper

❶ Heat oven to 300°F. Spray 9-inch springform pan with nonstick cooking spray.

❷ Sprinkle inside of pan with bread crumbs and ¼ cup of the Parmesan. Shake crumbs around sides and bottom of pan until well coated.

❸ In large skillet, melt butter over medium-high heat. Add onion and green onions; sauté until tender but not brown. Set aside.

❹ In large bowl, combine cream cheese, eggs and cream; beat at medium speed until smooth. Stir in onions, salmon, salt and pepper. Pour mixture into pan. Wrap bottom with aluminum foil. Place pan in large pan filled 1 inch deep with hot water. Bake 1 hour 40 minutes.

❺ Turn off oven; leave cheesecake inside 1 hour. Remove cake from water bath; place on wire rack to cool 45 to 60 minutes. Refrigerate in pan overnight. Remove from pan; serve with bagels.

20 servings.

SMOKED SALMON CHEESECAKE

CHEESY HASH BROWNS

KAREN SWARTZ
ST. ALLEGAN, MICHIGAN

These potatoes will disappear at family get-togethers. They are great for brunch or dinner.

1   (2-lb.) bag frozen hash browns, thawed
½   cup butter, cut up
2   cups sour cream
1   (10¾-oz.) can cream of mushroom soup
2¼ cups (9 oz.) shredded cheddar cheese
1   teaspoon salt
¼   teaspoon freshly ground pepper

❶ Heat oven to 350°F. Spray 13x9-inch pan with nonstick cooking spray.

❷ In large bowl, combine hash browns, butter, sour cream, soup, cheddar, salt and pepper; mix well. Spoon mixture into pan. Bake 1 to 1¼ hours or until top is lightly golden.

12 servings.

SILVER DOLLAR PANCAKES WITH WALNUTS

FANNIE KLINE
MILLERSBURG, OHIO

Holiday brunch or weekend guests all enjoy a good homemade pancake. This is my favorite to make and eat.

1   cup all-purpose flour
¼   cup toasted wheat germ
1   teaspoon baking soda
1   teaspoon salt
1   teaspoon packed brown sugar
    Dash ground cinnamon
1   cup buttermilk
1   egg
¼   cup walnuts
    Butter (optional)
    Maple syrup (optional)

❶ In blender, combine flour, wheat germ, baking soda, salt, brown sugar, cinnamon, buttermilk and egg; blend 15 seconds. Scrape sides of blender; add walnuts. Blend until walnuts are chopped fine, but not too fine.

❷ Put a few drops vegetable oil on large griddle; heat until hot. Pour batter onto griddle to make small pancakes. Cook each pancake 1½ minutes or until golden brown on both sides. Serve with butter and maple syrup, if desired. Batter may be prepared a day in advance and stored, covered, in refrigerator.

About 10 pancakes.

CHOCOLATE CHIP PANCAKES

TOMMIE COULTER
FORNEY, TEXAS

I make these for my daughter on cloudy days. They're sure to brighten up anyone's day.

1¼ cups all-purpose flour
1   tablespoon baking powder
1   tablespoon sugar
1   teaspoon ground cinnamon
½   teaspoon salt
1   cup half-and-half
2   tablespoons vegetable oil
1   teaspoon vanilla
1   egg
½   cup miniature semisweet chocolate chips
    Butter (optional)
    Maple syrup (optional)

❶ In large bowl, sift together flour, baking powder, sugar, cinnamon and salt. In medium bowl, combine half-and-half, oil, vanilla and egg; mix well. Add egg mixture to dry ingredients; mix with fork, leaving some lumps. Gently fold in chocolate chips. Cook pancakes on hot griddle. Serve with butter and warm maple syrup, if desired.

About 12 pancakes.

SWEDISH PANCAKES (UNGSPANKAKA)

KIMBERLY SWANSON
COLLBRAN, COLORADO

Grandma used to make these on Christmas Day when we were little. I was more excited about the pancakes than the presents!

4   eggs, beaten
2   cups milk
2   tablespoons butter, melted
1¼ cups all-purpose flour
1   tablespoon sugar
1   teaspoon salt
    Butter (optional)
    Syrup (optional)

❶ Heat oven to 425°F. Spray 13x9-inch pan with nonstick cooking spray.

❷ In large bowl, combine eggs, milk, melted butter, flour, sugar and salt; mix well. Pour batter into pan. Bake 15 to 20 minutes or until lightly browned. Serve with butter and syrup, if desired.

4 to 6 servings.

GERMAN PANCAKES (EIERKUCHEN)

CAROLE LINDSEY-POTTER
GREENSBORO, NORTH CAROLINA

I ate these pancakes as a child at my grandmother's house on Sunday mornings. Now I make them for my children.

1	cup all-purpose flour
¼	teaspoon baking soda
¼	teaspoon baking powder
	Dash salt
½	cup buttermilk
6	eggs, separated
1	tablespoon granulated sugar
1	teaspoon vanilla
2	tablespoons sour cream
	Dash cream of tartar
	Powdered sugar (optional)
	Jelly (optional)

❶ In large bowl, combine flour, baking soda, baking powder, salt and ¼ cup of the buttermilk. Add egg yolks, granulated sugar and vanilla; beat at medium speed until smooth. Add remaining ¼ cup buttermilk and sour cream; mix well. In medium bowl, add cream of tartar to egg whites; beat until stiff. Fold egg whites into batter. Heat griddle; grease with butter. Spoon batter onto griddle to crepe thickness. Cook until light brown on both sides. Serve with powdered sugar or jelly if desired.

4 servings.

WAFFLES

CAROLYN LUMSDEN
DRESSER, WISCONSIN

I've been making this recipe for 41 years. My mother-in-law gave it to me and I've shared it with a new bride.

3	eggs, separated
2	cups all-purpose flour
1	teaspoon baking powder
1	teaspoon salt
½	cup shortening, melted
2	cups milk

❶ In medium bowl, beat egg whites until stiff peaks form. In another medium bowl, combine flour, baking powder, salt, shortening, egg yolks and milk; mix well. Fold egg whites into batter. Heat waffle iron; spray with nonstick cooking spray. Pour batter into iron; close and bake until light brown, according to manufacturer's directions. For crisper waffles, extend cooking time.

12 (4-inch) waffles.

BAKED APPLE FRENCH TOAST

TERESA BELL
PITTSBURGH, PENNSYLVANIA

Here's a quick, no-fuss recipe for French toast lovers who are on the go in the morning!

1	cup packed brown sugar
⅓	cup butter
2	tablespoons corn syrup
½	teaspoon ground cinnamon
4	cups apples, peeled, sliced
1	tablespoon tapioca
4	eggs
1	cup milk
1	teaspoon vanilla
	Dash salt
12	(1-inch-thick) slices French bread

❶ In microwave-safe bowl, combine brown sugar, butter, corn syrup and cinnamon. Microwave on High 2 minutes or until butter is melted. Pour mixture into 13x9-inch pan. Arrange apples neatly on top. Sprinkle tapioca over apples.

❷ In medium bowl, combine eggs, milk, vanilla and salt; mix well. Soak bread in milk mixture; lay over apples. Cover; refrigerate 24 hours. Heat oven to 350°F. Bake uncovered 35 to 40 minutes.

12 servings.

OATMEAL WAFFLES

OATMEAL WAFFLES

SHARON FLANAGAN
MISSISSAUGA, ONTARIO, CANADA

Here's my family's favorite waffle recipe.

1½ cups all-purpose flour
1 cup quick cooking oats
1 tablespoon baking powder
¼ teaspoon ground cinnamon
¼ teaspoon ground nutmeg
½ to ¾ cup chopped fresh fruit or nuts of choice
1½ cups milk
2 eggs, lightly beaten
6 tablespoons canola or olive oil
2 tablespoons packed brown sugar
Fresh fruit (optional)
Maple syrup (optional)

❶ In large bowl, combine flour, oats, baking powder, cinnamon, nutmeg and fruit or nuts.

❷ In another large bowl, combine milk, eggs, oil and brown sugar; mix well. Carefully mix in flour mixture.

❸ Heat waffle iron; spray with nonstick cooking spray. Pour batter into iron; close and bake until light brown, according to manufacturer's directions. For crisper waffles, extend cooking time. Top with fresh fruit or maple syrup, if desired.

About 4 (9-inch) waffles.

GLAZED POTATO DOUGHNUTS

TAMI ZYLKA
BLUE BELL, PENNSYLVANIA

This is my maternal grandmother's recipe. She raised eight children while helping my grandfather on the farm, and still had time to make these almost every Saturday morning.

BATTER
1 (¼-oz.) pkg. active dry yeast
¼ cup warm water (105° to 115°F)
1 cup milk, scalded
¼ cup shortening
¼ cup granulated sugar
1 teaspoon salt
¾ cup mashed potatoes
2 eggs, beaten
5 to 6 cups all-purpose flour, sifted

GLAZE
1 (1-lb.) pkg. powdered sugar
6 tablespoons water
1 tablespoon vanilla

❶ For Batter: In small bowl, dissolve yeast in warm water; cool until lukewarm. In large bowl, combine scalded milk, shortening, granulated sugar and salt. Stir in yeast mixture, potatoes and eggs. Gradually add enough flour, 1 cup at a time, to make soft dough. Turn dough out onto floured surface; knead until smooth and satiny.

❷ Place in lightly greased bowl, turning once to grease top. Cover; let rise in warm place, away from drafts, until doubled in size. Roll dough to ½ inch thick; cut with 3-inch doughnut cutter. Cover; let rise in warm place, away from drafts, until doubled, about 30 minutes.

❸ For Glaze: In medium bowl, combine powdered sugar, water and vanilla; stir until mixture resembles thick cream. Heat deep fryer to 375°F. Drop 1 doughnut into deep fryer; cook, turning once, 4 to 5 minutes or until lightly browned. Remove doughnut to paper towels; drain. Roll hot doughnut in glaze. Place on wire rack until glaze sets. Repeat with remaining dough.

12 doughnuts.

SAUSAGE BREAD

ANITA COYNE
BONITA SPRINGS, FLORIDA

This is always requested for our family get-togethers.

1   (1-lb.) loaf frozen bread dough, thawed
8   oz. hot pork sausage, cooked, crumbled
1   medium onion, sliced
1   cup (4 oz.) shredded cheddar cheese

❶ Divide dough in half. Roll each half into 8x4-inch rectangle. Cover; let stand 15 minutes.

❷ Meanwhile, in medium skillet, sauté sausage and onion over medium heat until browned; drain. Roll each dough half into 12x8-inch rectangle. Spread ½ of sausage mixture and ½ cup cheddar evenly onto each loaf. Roll up jelly-roll fashion; seal ends. Spray each loaf with nonstick cooking spray.

❸ Heat oven to 350°F. Spray 15x10x1-inch baking pan with nonstick cooking spray. Let loaves rise in warm place, away from drafts, until doubled, about 1 hour. Bake 30 to 35 minutes or until bread is browned and sounds hollow when tapped. Let cool 5 minutes. Remove loaves to wire racks. Slice; serve at room temperature or reheated in oven.

6 to 8 servings.

RICOTTA FRITTERS

DOLORES IOVINO
RIVERSIDE, ILLINOIS

My mother often made these fritters for me. The recipe was handed down to her by her family.

3   eggs, beaten
¼   cup sugar, plus more for coating
½   teaspoon vanilla
1   teaspoon grated orange or lemon peel
¼   teaspoon grated nutmeg
12   oz. ricotta cheese
1¼   cups self-rising flour

❶ Heat deep fryer to 325°F.

❷ In medium bowl, combine eggs, ¼ cup sugar, vanilla, orange peel and nutmeg; mix well. Stir in ricotta and flour until well blended. Drop 1 tablespoon batter into deep fryer; cook, turning once, 4 or 5 minutes or until lightly browned. Remove fritter to paper towels; drain. Roll hot fritter in granulated sugar. Repeat with remaining batter.

38 fritters.

CRUMB CAKE

MARGARET DOHERTY
OAK RIDGE, TENNESSEE

I've been married for 56 years and have made good use of this recipe. I gave each of our five daughters this recipe to take into her marriage.

3   cups all-purpose flour
2   cups granulated sugar
2   teaspoons baking powder
1   teaspoon salt
1   cup butter
2   eggs
½   cup milk
½   teaspoon ground cinnamon
    Powdered sugar for sprinkling

❶ Heat oven to 375°F. Spray 13x9-inch pan with nonstick cooking spray.

❷ In medium bowl, combine flour, granulated sugar, baking powder, salt and ½ cup of the butter; mix well with fork. Reserve 2½ cups of mixture. To mixture remaining in bowl, add eggs and milk; mix until stiff batter forms. Pour batter into pan. To reserved mixture, add cinnamon and remaining ½ cup butter; mix well. Pour reserved mixture over batter. Bake 30 to 35 minutes. Remove cake from oven; sprinkle with powdered sugar.

16 servings.

TOFFEE BAR COFFEE CAKE

CHRISTINE JONES
AKRON, OHIO

My siblings and I loved this treat as kids. I received the recipe on a plaque for a wedding shower gift. It's now an equally special treat for my kids.

2   cups all-purpose flour
1   cup granulated sugar
½   cup packed brown sugar
    Dash salt
½   cup butter, cut up
1   teaspoon baking soda
1   cup buttermilk
1   teaspoon vanilla
1   egg
6   to 8 snack-size English toffee bars, crumbled

❶ Heat oven to 350°F. Spray 13x9-inch pan with nonstick cooking spray; lightly flour.

❷ In large bowl, combine flour, granulated sugar, brown sugar, salt and butter; mix well. Reserve ½ cup of batter for topping. Add baking soda, buttermilk, vanilla and egg to batter left in bowl; mix well. Pour batter into pan. In another bowl, combine reserved batter and toffee bars; mix until well coated. Pour over batter in pan. Bake 30 to 35 minutes. Serve warm; refrigerate any leftovers.

16 servings.

HOLIDAY CHEER COFFEE CAKE

MARILYN GRAESSER
CHICO, CALIFORNIA

When my children return home with their own families for the holidays, they always ask for this cake that reminds them of their childhood holidays.

¼   cup chopped nuts
¼   cup packed brown sugar
1   teaspoon ground cinnamon
1   (18-oz.) pkg. yellow cake mix
3   (¾-oz.) pkg. vanilla pudding mix
4   eggs
1   cup sour cream
½   cup white wine
1   teaspoon vanilla

❶ Heat oven to 350°F. Spray 12-cup Bundt pan with nonstick cooking spray; lightly flour. In small bowl, combine nuts, brown sugar and cinnamon; set aside.

❷ In large bowl, combine cake mix, pudding mix, eggs, sour cream, wine and vanilla; beat at medium speed 3 minutes. Pour half of the batter into pan. Spread nut mixture evenly over batter; top with remaining batter. Bake 45 to 50 minutes. Cool 10 to 15 minutes before serving.

16 servings.

WALNUT ROLL

SVETLANA DZHANGIROVA
SEATTLE, WASHINGTON

This roll is one of my specialties. On Easter, my family and friends enjoy it so much they can't eat just one piece.

BATTER
1   (¼-oz.) pkg. active dry yeast
1   cup warm milk (105°F to 115°F)
6   tablespoons sugar
½   cup butter, softened
½   teaspoon salt
4   eggs, at room temperature
4   cups all-purpose flour

FILLING
3   cups ground walnuts
1½ cups sugar
1   teaspoon ground cinnamon
¼   teaspoon ground nutmeg
5   tablespoons (3 oz.) honey, warmed
1   egg yolk, lightly beaten

❶ For Batter: In large bowl, dissolve yeast in warm milk. Add 6 tablespoons sugar, let stand 5 minutes. Add 5 tablespoons of the butter and salt; set aside until warm and butter almost melts. Add eggs and 2 cups of the flour; beat at medium speed until smooth. Stir in enough remaining flour, 1 cup at a time, until soft dough forms. Turn dough out onto lightly floured surface; knead until smooth, 6 to 8 minutes.

❷ Place dough in lightly greased bowl; turn once. Cover; let rise in warm place, away from drafts, until doubled in size, about 1 hour. Punch dough down. Turn onto lightly floured surface; divide in half. Cover; let rest 10 to 15 minutes.

❸ For Filling: In clean large bowl, combine walnuts, 1½ cups sugar, cinnamon, nutmeg and honey; mix well. Divide in half; set aside. On lightly floured surface, roll ½ of the dough into 15x10-inch rectangle. In microwave, melt remaining 3 tablespoons butter. Brush half of the melted butter over dough. Spread half of the filling evenly over rectangle. Roll up from 1 of the long sides; seal seams and ends. Place loaf on greased 15x10x1-inch baking pan. Repeat with remaining dough, butter and walnut mixture. Cover; let rise until nearly doubled, about 30 minutes. Heat oven to 375°F. Brush rolls with egg yolk. Prick with fork a few times along each roll. Bake 25 to 30 minutes. Cool slightly; slice. Arrange slices on large serving plate.

2 loaves.

ANN ZYLKA'S SPONGE PLACEK (POLISH COFFEE BREAD)

TAMI ZYLKA
BLUE BELL, PENNSYLVANIA

This recipe is from my mother-in-law. It is made for Easter and Christmas in Polish households.

BATTER
2   cups lukewarm milk
2   tablespoons plus 1¾ cups sugar
1   (¼-oz.) pkg. active dry yeast
6   cups all-purpose flour
1   cup butter, melted
5   eggs
1   teaspoon salt
1   tablespoon whiskey
1   teaspoon vanilla

TOPPING
½   cup butter, softened
1½ cups all-purpose flour
½   cup sugar

❶ For Batter: In large bowl, combine lukewarm milk, 2 tablespoons of the sugar, yeast and 3 cups of the flour. Let rise 30 minutes or until mixture starts to rise and bubble.

❷ In large bowl, add melted butter, 1¾ cups sugar, eggs, salt, whiskey, vanilla and 3 cups flour. Spray 2 (9x5-inch) loaf pans with nonstick cooking spray. Pour mixture into pans.

❸ For Topping: In medium bowl, combine softened butter, 1½ cups flour and ½ cup sugar; mix well. Pour mixture into pans. Let rise 1 hour. Heat oven to 375°F. Bake 35 to 40 minutes.

2 loaves.

OVERNIGHT PECAN ROLLS

CAROL HAWLEY
FREDERICK, MARYLAND

I have been making these for a number of years for our overnight guests.

BATTER
2   (¼-oz.) pkg. active dry yeast
½   cup warm water (105°F to 115°F)
2   cups warm milk (105°F to 115°F)
⅓   cup granulated sugar
⅓   cup vegetable oil
1   tablespoon baking powder
1   teaspoon salt
1   egg
6½ to 7½ cups flour

FILLING
½   cup butter
1   cup packed brown sugar
2   tablespoons corn syrup
1   cup pecan halves
½   cup granulated sugar
4   teaspoons ground cinnamon
¼   cup butter, melted

FROSTING
1   lb. butter, at room temperature
2   (8-oz.) pkg. cream cheese, at room temperature
2   lb. powdered sugar
2   teaspoons lemon juice
2   teaspoons vanilla

❶ For Batter: In large bowl, dissolve yeast in warm water. Stir in warm milk, ⅓ cup granulated sugar, oil, baking powder, salt, egg and 3 cups of the flour; beat at medium speed until smooth. Add enough remaining flour, 1 cup at a time, until dough is easy to handle. Place dough in large greased bowl. Cover; let rise in warm place, away from drafts, 1½ hours.

❷ For Filling: In medium saucepan, heat ½ cup butter and brown sugar; stir to dissolve. Remove from heat; stir in corn syrup. Divide mixture between 2 (13x9-inch) pans. Sprinkle with pecans. In small bowl, combine ½ cup granulated sugar and cinnamon. Divide dough in half; roll each half into 12x10-inch rectangle. Spread each evenly with melted butter and cinnamon mixture. Roll up from long sides; cut each into 12 (1-inch) slices. Place in pan; cover with aluminum foil. Refrigerate 12 to 48 hours.

❸ Heat oven to 350°F. Remove dough from refrigerator. Bake covered 30 minutes. Meanwhile, prepare Frosting: In clean large bowl, mix 1 lb. butter and cream cheese. Slowly add powdered sugar; continue mixing 10 minutes. Add lemon juice and vanilla; mix 2 minutes. When rolls are done, immediately remove from oven; invert onto aluminum foil. Spread frosting over rolls.

2 dozen rolls.

OVERNIGHT PECAN ROLLS

GRANDMA'S CHOCOLATE CAKE
JANICE GOODNER
MACOMB, OKLAHOMA

My grandma used to make this cake; because I loved it so much as a child, I still make it today.

CAKE
1   cup buttermilk
¾   cup canola oil
2   eggs
2   cups sugar
2   teaspoons baking soda
½   teaspoon salt
1   tablespoon vanilla
2   cups unbleached all-purpose flour
½   cup unsweetened cocoa
1   cup very hot water

FROSTING
1   cup sugar
½   cup unsweetened cocoa
    Dash salt
¼   cup butter
¼   cup whipping cream or evaporated milk
1   teaspoon vanilla

❶ Heat oven to 350°F. Spray 13x9-inch pan with nonstick cooking spray.

❷ For Cake: In large bowl, beat buttermilk, oil, eggs, 2 cups sugar, baking soda, ½ teaspoon salt and 1 tablespoon vanilla at medium speed. In small bowl, sift together flour and ½ cup cocoa; stir into buttermilk mixture. Slowly pour in hot water. Pour batter into pan. Bake 25 to 30 minutes. Remove when toothpick inserted near center comes out clean. Cool pan on wire rack.

❸ Meanwhile, prepare Frosting: In medium saucepan, combine 1 cup sugar, ½ cup cocoa and dash salt. Add butter and cream; bring to a boil, stirring over medium-high heat. Boil 1 minute. Remove from heat; stir in 1 teaspoon vanilla. Pour over cooled cake.

12 servings.

CINNAMON TOAST COFFEE CAKE
CHARLOTTE WARD
HILTON HEAD ISLAND, SOUTH CAROLINA

This is one of our traditional Christmas morning brunch items. As our children were growing up, it was one of their favorite foods year-round — morning, noon and night.

2   cups all-purpose flour
1½   cups sugar
2   teaspoons baking powder
1   teaspoon salt
1   cup milk
2   tablespoons plus ½ cup butter, melted
1   teaspoon vanilla
½   cup raisins
1½   teaspoons ground cinnamon

❶ Heat oven to 350°F. Spray 15x10x1-inch baking pan with nonstick cooking spray; lightly flour.

❷ In large bowl, sift together flour, 1 cup of the sugar, baking powder and salt. Blend in milk, 2 tablespoons of the butter, vanilla and raisins; mix well. Turn mixture into pan. Bake 20 to 25 minutes or until golden brown. Drizzle with remaining ½ cup butter.

❸ In small bowl, combine remaining ½ cup sugar and cinnamon; sprinkle over cake. Bake 10 minutes. Cut into squares.

12 servings.

STARTERS

MUSHROOM CRESCENTS

MARLIS HOUGHTON
COOS BAY, OREGON

These are great if you're hosting an after-work happy hour.

1   (8-oz.) pkg. plus 3 oz. cream cheese, softened
¾   cup butter, at room temperature
1½ cups all-purpose flour
1   medium onion, chopped
8   oz. mushrooms, chopped
½   teaspoon salt
¼   teaspoon dried thyme
⅛   teaspoon white pepper
1   egg, beaten
1   teaspoon water

❶ In large bowl, with wooden spoon, combine 8 oz. of the cream cheese, ½ cup plus 2 tablespoons of the butter and flour until smooth. Cover; refrigerate at least 30 minutes. Heat oven to 450°F.

❷ In large skillet, heat remaining 2 tablespoons butter over medium-high heat until hot. Add onion; sauté until lightly brown. Add mushrooms; cook 3 minutes. Reduce heat; add remaining 3 oz. cream cheese, a bit at a time, stirring until melted. Stir in salt, thyme and white pepper. Remove from heat; cool.

❸ Remove half of the dough from refrigerator. On floured board, roll dough ⅛ inch thick. Cut into 2½-inch circles. Place ½ teaspoon mushroom filling on each circle, fold in half, pressing edges with fork. Cut small slit in top of each crescent. Repeat with remaining dough and filling. In small bowl, combine egg and water; brush over each crescent. Arrange crescents on baking sheet. Bake 15 minutes; cool.

50 crescents.

BAKED POTATO SALAD

BRANDI ROBINSON
CONROE, TEXAS

This is one of my favorite side dishes. It is simple, tasty and wonderful to eat.

5   lb. red potatoes, cubed, cooked
¼   cup butter
6   to 8 thick slices bacon, fried, crumbled
1¼ cups (5 oz.) shredded colby jack cheese
⅓   cup chopped green onions
1   (8-oz.) container sour cream

❶ In large bowl, lightly mash potatoes with fork. Add butter, bacon, colby jack and green onions; mix well. Serve with sour cream.

8 servings.

WHITE CHEESE AND TOMATO TART

BARBARA NOWAKOWSKI
NORTH TONAWANDA, NEW YORK

These are incredible!

CRUST
2   cups all-purpose flour
½   teaspoon salt
¾   cup shortening
5   to 6 tablespoons cold water

FILLING
2   cups (8 oz.) shredded Gruyère cheese
½   cup all-purpose flour
¼   cup butter
1   teaspoon salt
½   teaspoon white pepper
1   (15-oz.) container ricotta cheese
2   eggs
6   plum tomatoes, sliced
    Fresh dill weed (optional)

❶ Heat oven to 475°F. For Crust: In large bowl, combine flour and salt. With pastry blender, cut in shortening until mixture crumbles. Sprinkle in cold water, 1 tablespoon at a time, until pastry pulls away from sides of bowl. Gather pastry into ball; shape into flattened round on lightly floured surface. Roll pastry 2 inches larger than tart pan with removable bottom. Ease pastry into pan; prick bottom and sides of pastry with fork. Bake 15 minutes or until set; cool. Reduce oven temperature to 375°F.

❷ For Filling: In food processor, combine Gruyère, flour, butter, salt, white pepper, ricotta and eggs. Process 1 minute or until smooth. Spoon filling into cooled crust. Top with tomato slices. Bake 35 to 40 minutes or until top is light brown. Cool; remove pan sides. Cut tart into 1½-inch squares. Garnish with dill, if desired.

24 servings.

ROASTED GARLIC AND SPINACH SPIRALS

BARBARA NOWAKOWSKI
NORTH TONAWANDA, NEW YORK

My friends always hope these will be on my party table ... and they always are!

1   bulb garlic
3   cups spinach leaves, rinsed, patted dry
1   (15-oz.) can white beans, drained, rinsed
1   teaspoon dried oregano
¼   teaspoon freshly ground pepper
⅛   teaspoon cayenne pepper
7   (8-inch) flour tortillas

❶ Heat oven to 400°F. Trim top of garlic just enough to cut tips off center cloves; discard tips. Moisten head of garlic with water; wrap in aluminum foil. Bake 45 minutes or until garlic is soft and has mellow aroma; cool. Remove garlic from skin by squeezing between fingers and thumb; place garlic in food processor. Finely shred spinach by stacking and cutting several leaves at a time. Place in medium bowl; set aside.

❷ To garlic in food processor, add beans, oregano, ground pepper and cayenne; process until smooth. Add spinach; mix well. Spread mixture evenly on tortillas; roll up. Trim ½ inch off ends of rolls; discard trimmings. Cut rolls into 1-inch pieces to serve.

10 servings.

CHEESE PUFFS

SANDRA BODENDIECK
ST. LOUIS, MISSOURI

My friend Shirley shared this recipe with me many years ago when we'd celebrate New Year's Eve with each other's families. Many a happy memory was made with these little cheese puffs.

1   (8-oz.) pkg. shredded cheddar cheese
½   cup butter or margarine, softened
1   cup all-purpose flour
1   teaspoon paprika
½   teaspoon salt
48 small pimiento-stuffed green olives

❶ Spray 15x10x1-inch baking pan with nonstick cooking spray. In large bowl, blend cheddar and butter. Stir in flour, paprika and salt; mix well. Coat each olive completely with 1 teaspoon mixture. Arrange on pan about 1 inch apart; refrigerate 30 minutes or until firm. Bake 15 minutes at 400°F.

4 dozen cheese puffs.

MOTHER MASEMER'S FAMOUS POTATO SALAD

LUANN SHUTTS
KIRBY, TEXAS

Anyone who has ever eaten Shirley Masemer's potato salad knows that the bowl is always empty well before the end of the gathering.

5   medium potatoes, cooked, cooled, peeled and
      cut into 1-inch cubes
3   ribs celery, finely chopped
¼   cup finely chopped onion
2   cups mayonnaise
¼   cup vinegar
3   tablespoons prepared mustard
¾   cup sugar
1   tablespoon mustard seeds
1   tablespoon celery seed

❶ In large bowl, combine potatoes, celery and onion; mix gently. Set aside. In small bowl, combine mayonnaise, vinegar, prepared mustard and sugar; mix well. Gently stir half of the vinegar mixture into potato mixture, tossing gently until potatoes are coated. Keep adding remaining dressing until salad is moist. Sprinkle mustard seeds and celery seed into salad. Store in refrigerator.

12 servings.

POTATO SALAD

BARBARA BARTOLOMEO
RADNOR, PENNSYLVANIA

I've been eating potato salad all my life. Here's my mom's recipe, the best of all.

5   lb. large red potatoes, cooked, peeled and
       cut into ½-inch cubes
2   cups diced celery
2   cups chopped onion
¾   cup diced green bell pepper
1   large bunch parsley, finely chopped
1½   cups mayonnaise
3   tablespoons water
2   tablespoons red wine vinegar
¼   teaspoon sugar
⅛   teaspoon salt
⅛   teaspoon freshly ground pepper
     Paprika

❶ In large bowl, combine potatoes, celery, onion, bell pepper and parsley. In medium bowl, combine mayonnaise, water, vinegar, sugar, salt and ground pepper; stir until smooth. Add vinegar mixture to potato mixture, tossing gently until potatoes are coated. Refrigerate at least 2 hours before serving. Sprinkle with paprika. Store in refrigerator.

16 servings.

LUMPIA

LUMPIA

KAZ AND JOY LOCKHART
TYLER, TEXAS

My Japanese sister-in-law brings these to our family gatherings. She serves them alongside a wonderful sauce made of soy sauce and mustard.

½ lb. ground pork
½ lb. shelled, deveined uncooked medium shrimp, finely chopped
½ cup mushrooms, finely chopped
¼ cup water chestnuts, finely chopped
2 tablespoons finely chopped fresh chives
½ teaspoon salt
⅛ teaspoon freshly ground pepper
1 tablespoon soy sauce
1 egg yolk
36 wonton wrappers
1 tablespoon cornstarch
½ cup water
Vegetable oil

❶ In large bowl, combine pork, shrimp, mushrooms, water chestnuts, chives, salt, pepper, soy sauce and egg yolk. Place 1 tablespoon of mixture on each wrapper. In small bowl, combine cornstarch and water. With fingers, brush mixture over edges of wrappers; fold wrappers to seal. Deep-fry until Lumpia are golden brown; drain well. These can be pre-fried and reheated at 400°F 10 minutes.

12 servings.

MUSTARD BEAN SALAD

DAVID RITTER
DOUGLASSVILLE, PENNSYLVANIA

My wife Patty and I both enjoyed mustard bean salads when we were younger. This is our modern adaptation of a classic, suitable for a summer picnic with friends and family.

2 lb. yellow string beans, rinsed, cut into 1-inch lengths
¼ cup finely chopped onion
¼ cup country-style Dijon mustard
2 tablespoons vinegar

❶ In medium pot, cook beans in water over medium-high heat until slightly firm, about 7 minutes. Cool slightly; drain, reserving 3 tablespoons water for dressing.

❷ Meanwhile, in large bowl, combine onion, Dijon, vinegar and reserved cooking liquid, 1 tablespoon at a time, until mixture is creamy. Add dressing to hot beans; toss gently. (Beans should be hot when dressing is added so that they absorb dressing flavor better.)

8 servings.

BLUEBERRY SALAD

KARLA MEEHAN
CHAMPAIGN, ILLINOIS

I first made this recipe in the 8th grade home economics class that started my love of cooking. I've adapted this salad over the years, and usually serve it at summer gatherings.

2 (3-oz.) pkg. raspberry gelatin
2 cups boiling water
1½ cups cold water
1 (¼-oz.) envelope unflavored gelatin
1 cup cream or half-and-half
1 cup sugar
1 teaspoon vanilla
1 (8-oz.) pkg. cream cheese, softened
½ cup pecans, chopped
1 (16-oz.) can blueberries with juice

❶ Dissolve 1 package of the raspberry gelatin in 1 cup of the boiling water and 1 cup of the cold water; pour into 8-inch square pan. Chill 4 hours or until set.

❷ In large bowl, dissolve unflavored gelatin in remaining ½ cup cold water. In small saucepan, heat cream and sugar; add to unflavored gelatin. Stir in vanilla. Beat in cream cheese with electric mixer at medium speed until smooth. Add pecans. Pour cream cheese mixture over set gelatin. Refrigerate 3 hours or until set.

❸ Dissolve remaining package raspberry gelatin in remaining 1 cup hot water. Mix in blueberries with juice; pour over second set layer. Refrigerate salad overnight. Store in refrigerator.

9 servings.

CRANBERRY RIBBON SALAD MOLD

LINDA MANIA
OCALA, FLORIDA

Here's one of our family's favorite holiday recipes.

1   (¼-oz.) envelope unflavored gelatin
1   cup cold water
1   (3-oz.) pkg. cranberry or raspberry gelatin
¾   cup boiling water
1   (14-oz.) container cranberry-orange relish
¼   cup lemon juice
1   teaspoon grated orange peel
1   (8-oz.) pkg. cream cheese, softened
1   (6½-oz.) container frozen whipped topping, thawed

❶ In small saucepan, sprinkle unflavored gelatin over cold water to dissolve; heat over medium heat, stirring occasionally. Remove from heat; set aside.

❷ In medium bowl, dissolve cranberry gelatin in boiling water. Stir in relish, 2 tablespoons of the lemon juice and orange peel. Pour into 1½-quart gelatin mold. Refrigerate until thickened. In large mixing bowl beat cream cheese with remaining 2 tablespoons lemon juice until fluffy. Mix in whipped topping. Add unflavored gelatin. Spoon mixture evenly over set gelatin. Refrigerate 3 hours or until set. Store in refrigerator.

8 servings.

STRAWBERRY-SPINACH SALAD

JANELLE BEECHER
FOND DU LAC, WISCONSIN

A friend of the family brought this summery salad to a gathering a few years back. It instantly became a family favorite. It's simple to make and is so light and fresh.

1   bunch fresh spinach leaves (about 6 cups), rinsed, dried and torn into bite-size pieces
2   cups strawberries, sliced
⅓   cup sugar
¼   to ½ teaspoon dry mustard
¼   cup red wine vinegar
2   tablespoons olive oil
1   teaspoon poppy seeds

❶ In large bowl, toss spinach and strawberries. In medium bowl, combine sugar, mustard, vinegar, oil and poppy seeds; mix well. Pour dressing over salad; toss before serving.

6 servings.

HOLIDAY EGGNOG

PEGGY POINTER
KETTERING, OHIO

This cooked version of eggnog helps us avoid raw eggs and still enjoy this Yuletide treat. It is foolproof if you use an instant-read thermometer. This eliminates the guesswork of determining when you have reached the "coats the spoon" stage.

4   cups half-and-half
1   cup whipping cream
¾   cup sugar
7   extra-large or 9 large egg yolks
1   tablespoon vanilla
½   teaspoon freshly grated nutmeg
1   cup milk, for thinning eggnog if needed

❶ In large saucepan, combine half-and-half, cream, sugar and egg yolks; whisk until well-combined. Cook over medium heat, continuing to whisk 8 to 10 minutes, or until thermometer reads 170°F. Remove from heat, beating mixture until slightly cooled. Stir in vanilla and nutmeg. Transfer eggnog to bowl or pitcher. Cover; refrigerate 8 hours or up to 2 days. Just before serving, thin with milk if needed.

About 1½ quarts.

HOT CRAB DIP

JENNIFER OKUTMAN
WESTMINSTER, MARYLAND

This is a great holiday appetizer.

1   lb. lump crabmeat
2   (8-oz.) pkg. cream cheese, softened
1   cup sour cream
¼   cup mayonnaise
    Juice of ½ lemon
1   tablespoon Worcestershire sauce
¼   teaspoon garlic powder
⅛   teaspoon cayenne pepper
½   cup grated cheddar cheese
    Old Bay seasoning

❶ Heat oven to 325°F. Spray 13x9-inch pan with nonstick cooking spray.

❷ In large bowl, combine crabmeat, cream cheese, sour cream, mayonnaise, lemon juice, Worcestershire, garlic powder, cayenne and cheddar; mix well. Sprinkle with Old Bay. Bake 30 to 40 minutes. Serve with crackers or French bread.

12 servings.

TRIPLE CHEESE APPETIZER CHEESECAKE

BARBARA NOWAKOWSKI
NORTH TONAWANDA, NEW YORK

I've been making this for years. It's delicious, serves many and is perfect for a buffet.

1   cup sesame crackers, crushed
3   tablespoons butter, softened
1   cup ricotta cheese
4   oz. feta cheese, finely crumbled
1   (8-oz.) pkg. cream cheese, softened
2   eggs
½   cup sour cream
½   cup roasted red bell peppers, chopped
2   tablespoons chopped fresh basil
¼   teaspoon garlic powder

❶ Heat oven to 350°F. In medium bowl, combine crushed crackers and butter; mix well. Press mixture into bottom and 1½ inches up sides of 9-inch springform pan.

❷ In large bowl, combine ricotta, feta and cream cheese; beat until creamy. Add eggs, one at a time, beating well after each addition. Stir in sour cream, roasted bell peppers, basil and garlic powder. Pour mixture into pan. Bake 35 to 40 minutes or until center is just about set. Remove pan from oven; cool 30 minutes. Loosen edges with small metal spatula or knife. Cool 30 minutes more or until completely cooled. Refrigerate at least 4 hours before serving. To serve, carefully remove pan sides; place pan base and cheesecake on serving plate. Cut into thin wedges; serve with assorted crackers. Store in refrigerator.

24 servings.

HOT VIDALIA ONION DIP

MOLLY RINDT
HAMPSTEAD, MARYLAND

This recipe brings fond memories of coming inside after playing outside as a kid.

3   cups finely chopped Vidalia onions
2   cups mayonnaise
2   cups (8 oz.) shredded Swiss cheese
¼   teaspoon hot pepper sauce
½   cup freshly grated Parmesan cheese

❶ Heat oven to 350°F. Spray 13x9-inch pan with nonstick cooking spray.

❷ In large bowl, combine onions, mayonnaise, Swiss cheese and hot pepper sauce; mix well. Spread mixture into pan; sprinkle with Parmesan. Bake 30 minutes until bubbly. Serve with veggies, crackers and chips.

8 servings.

JOY'S FORT LAUDERDALE SMOKED FISH DIP

JOY LOCKHART
TYLER, TEXAS

This is my personal take on Florida's famous fish dip.

½   lb. boneless skinless smoked marlin, flaked
4   oz. cream cheese
½   cup sour cream
2   tablespoons fresh lemon juice
2   teaspoons finely chopped fresh chives
1   teaspoon finely chopped fresh parsley
1   teaspoon finely chopped onion
½   teaspoon kosher (coarse) salt
⅛   teaspoon cayenne pepper
     Horseradish to taste
     Finely chopped capers to taste

❶ In large bowl, combine marlin, cream cheese, sour cream, lemon juice, chives, parsley, onion, salt, cayenne, horseradish and capers; mix well. (Thickness of dip can be adjusted by altering amounts of sour cream and cream cheese.) Cover; refrigerate at least 1 hour. Serve with assorted crackers.

2 cups.

MOM'S ARTICHOKE DIP

KRISTY SKORUPA
INDEPENDENCE, OHIO

This recipe is special because it reminds me of the holidays every time I make it. It also reminds me of my mother making it for me when I was little. It's simple to make and very delicious.

1   (14-oz.) can artichoke hearts, drained
1   (8-oz.) pkg. shredded mozzarella cheese
1   cup freshly grated Parmesan cheese
1   cup mayonnaise
     Dash garlic salt (optional)
1   tablespoon parsley (optional)

❶ Heat oven to 350°F. Spray 1-quart casserole with nonstick cooking spray.

❷ In large bowl, combine artichoke hearts, mozzarella, Parmesan, mayonnaise, garlic salt and parsley, if using; mix well. Spread mixture into casserole. Bake uncovered 30 minutes. Serve warm with tortilla chips or butter crackers.

8 servings.

KOREAN SALAD

VALERIE HOBBS
DEERFIELD, ILLINOIS

Here's my family's favorite salad recipe.

SALAD
1 (16-oz.) pkg. fresh spinach, washed, trimmed and drained
1 pint fresh mushrooms, sliced (2 cups)
1 (16-oz.) can bean sprouts, drained (2 cups)
1 (8-oz.) can sliced water chestnuts, drained
5 thick slices bacon, cooked, crumbled

DRESSING
1 cup vegetable oil
⅓ cup ketchup
¼ cup cider vinegar
½ cup sugar
1 very small red onion, grated

GARNISH
2 hard-cooked eggs, sliced (optional)

❶ For Salad: In large bowl, combine spinach, mushrooms, sprouts, water chestnuts and bacon; mix well.

❷ For Dressing: In food processor or blender, combine oil, ketchup, vinegar, sugar and onion; process until smooth. Pour dressing over salad; toss well. Garnish with egg slices, if desired.

8 to 12 servings.

MARINATED PRAWNS

KATJA COWIE
VANCOUVER, BRITISH COLUMBIA, CANADA

My family always asks for this great appetizer. It's light, refreshing and easy!

⅓ cup vegetable oil
¼ cup white wine vinegar
2 teaspoons fresh tarragon, chopped
1 teaspoon sugar
1 teaspoon Dijon mustard
2 garlic cloves, crushed
⅛ teaspoon salt
⅛ teaspoon freshly ground pepper
2 tablespoons chopped sun-dried tomatoes
12 to 18 shelled, deveined cooked jumbo shrimp, tails on

❶ In large resealable plastic bag, combine oil, vinegar, tarragon, sugar, Dijon, garlic, salt, pepper and tomatoes. Seal bag; shake to mix. Add shrimp; seal bag. Refrigerate overnight, turning bag occasionally.

4 servings.

BACON AND CHEESE DEVILED EGGS

DORIS HEDGES
WOODSTOCK, ILLINOIS

These eggs will disappear quickly. They were served at our "golden years" potluck.

12 hard-cooked eggs, peeled, halved lengthwise
½ cup mayonnaise
1 tablespoon Dijon mustard
½ teaspoon salt
¼ teaspoon freshly ground pepper
4 thick slices bacon, cooked, crumbled
2 tablespoons shredded sharp cheddar cheese
    Fresh parsley, for garnish

❶ Remove egg yolks to bowl, reserving whites. Mash yolks with fork. Add mayonnaise, Dijon, salt and pepper. Fold in bacon and cheddar. Fill egg white halves with yolk mixture; garnish with parsley. Cover; refrigerate until ready to serve.

12 servings.

MARINATED PRAWNS

ASPARAGUS WITH CITRUS VINAIGRETTE

ASPARAGUS WITH CITRUS VINAIGRETTE

DAVID RITTER
DOUGLASSVILLE, PENNSYLVANIA

Citrus, ginger and garlic are a great combination. This recipe is healthy and delicious.

¼ cup orange juice
2 tablespoons rice wine vinegar
4 teaspoons olive oil
1 tablespoon soy sauce
1 teaspoon grated fresh ginger
½ teaspoon finely chopped garlic
¼ teaspoon cayenne pepper
1 lb. asparagus, ends snapped off
¼ cup canned mandarin oranges, drained

❶ In large bowl, combine orange juice, vinegar, 1 tablespoon of the oil, soy sauce, ginger, garlic and cayenne; mix well. Let stand 30 minutes. Cut asparagus spears into 2-inch pieces.

❷ In medium skillet, heat remaining teaspoon oil over medium-high heat until hot. Add asparagus; stir-fry about 2 minutes. Stir orange juice mixture; pour over asparagus. Cook, stirring constantly, 2 to 4 minutes or until asparagus is crisp-tender. Stir in 2 tablespoons of the mandarin oranges. Transfer to serving bowl; top with remaining mandarin oranges. Serve immediately.

4 servings.

BLUE CHEESE DRESSING

CHARLOTTE WARD
HILTON HEAD ISLAND, SOUTH CAROLINA

According to my husband, "if it isn't blue cheese dressing, it isn't dressing." This has been his favorite for over 35 years.

1 cup mayonnaise
½ cup sour cream
¼ cup vinegar
1 tablespoon lemon juice
3 oz. blue cheese, crumbled

❶ In blender, combine mayonnaise, sour cream, vinegar and lemon juice; blend well. Pour mixture into large measuring cup. Stir in blue cheese; mix well. Serve over greens. Store in refrigerator up to 3 days.

1¾ cups.

STUFFED MUSHROOMS

JOAN YOUNG
AIKEN, SOUTH CAROLINA

In the 1970s, my aunt, who lived in Carmel, California, used to make this appetizer when we would visit. Today, my brothers and I still make it.

1 lb. large mushrooms
2 tablespoons butter
¼ cup finely minced onion
1 garlic clove, finely minced
2 tablespoons dry bread crumbs
2 tablespoons freshly grated Parmesan cheese
⅛ teaspoon salt
⅛ teaspoon freshly ground pepper
Dash dried oregano
½ cup ground beef
¼ cup olive oil

❶ Heat oven to 375°F. Reserve 12 large mushroom caps for stuffing. Remove stems of remaining mushrooms; chop. In large skillet, melt butter over medium-high heat. Add mushrooms; sauté 5 minutes. Add onion, garlic, bread crumbs, Parmesan, salt, pepper, oregano, beef and 1 tablespoon of the oil; cook 3 to 5 minutes. Stuff reserved mushroom caps with onion mixture; place in pan. Drizzle remaining 3 tablespoons oil over mushrooms. Bake 25 minutes.

12 stuffed mushrooms.

BROCCOLI SALAD

RAMONA KLOPPING
OMAHA, NEBRASKA

I prepare this easy and delicious salad for church dinners.

SALAD
4 to 6 cups chopped broccoli (florets and stems)
½ cup crumbled cooked bacon
½ cup raisins
½ cup diced onions
½ cup chopped walnuts

DRESSING
1 cup mayonnaise
2 tablespoons cider vinegar
¼ cup sugar

❶ For Salad: In large bowl, combine broccoli, bacon, raisins, onions and walnuts. For Dressing: In another large bowl, combine mayonnaise, vinegar and sugar; mix well. Pour dressing over salad; toss gently.

10 to 12 servings.

GARBANZO, FETA AND OLIVE SALAD

CYNDE LOPEZ
ALTO, NEW MEXICO

This salad is fresh tasting and always a big success when served. Don't be afraid to serve this with any entree; it's not just for Middle Eastern dishes.

1 (15-oz.) can garbanzo beans, drained, rinsed
½ cup crumbled feta cheese
½ cup sliced ripe olives
1 large tomato, seeded, diced
2 green onions, sliced
2 tablespoons finely chopped fresh parsley
1½ teaspoons olive oil
2 tablespoons red wine vinegar
⅛ teaspoon salt
⅛ teaspoon freshly ground pepper

❶ In large bowl, combine garbanzo beans, feta, olives, tomato, green onions and parsley; mix well. In small bowl, whisk together oil and vinegar. Pour over salad; toss well. Season with salt and pepper.

4 to 6 servings.

BRIDAL SHOWER PUNCH

VIVIAN NIKANOW
CHICAGO, ILLINOIS

I've made this punch numerous times. It is both sweet and tangy, and perfect for a shower. If you want to make it really fancy, freeze an ice ring mold filled with lemon-lime soda and fresh fruits, and place the ice ring in the punch. This keeps the punch cold but doesn't water it down.

1 (750-ml) bottle Champagne
1 (12-oz.) can frozen orange juice
1 (12-oz.) can frozen lemonade or limeade
1 (2-liter) bottle lemon-lime soda
  Sherbet of choice
  Fresh fruit of choice

❶ In punch bowl, combine Champagne, orange juice, lemonade and soda. Add sherbet as desired. Stir in fresh fruit.

About 4 quarts.

MAIN COURSES

SHRIMP AND LEEKS WITH PERNOD

WILLY WILKINS
RICHMOND HILL, ONTARIO, CANADA

Friday night is "fish night" in our family. We've been making this recipe for years.

6	tablespoons butter
2	leeks, chopped
2	tablespoons fresh dill, chopped, or 1 tablespoon dried
2	tablespoons dry white wine
1½	cups heavy cream
28	uncooked tiger shrimp
2	tablespoons Pernod or other anise-flavored liqueur

❶ In large saucepan, heat 2 tablespoons of the butter over medium heat. Add leeks and dill; cook about 3 minutes. Add wine; cook an additional 1 minute. Add cream; cook, stirring often, 5 to 7 minutes.

❷ As sauce reduces, in medium skillet, heat 2 tablespoons of the butter over medium heat. Add shrimp. Slowly add Pernod. Combine the 2 sauces; bring to a boil. Swirl in remaining 2 tablespoons butter.

4 servings.

CRAB CAKES

ROSE DeVITO
LONG BRANCH, NEW JERSEY

This recipe belonged to my late husband, Glenn, who was a chef and restaurant owner. It was a big hit in his restaurant, and my personal favorite.

½	cup mayonnaise
2	tablespoons Dijon mustard
¾	teaspoon Worcestershire sauce
½	cup fresh white bread crumbs
1½	teaspoons chopped fresh Italian parsley
3	green onions, chopped
⅛	teaspoon salt
⅛	teaspoon freshly ground pepper
1	lb. fresh jumbo lump crabmeat
1	cup all-purpose flour
½	cup olive oil

❶ In medium bowl, combine mayonnaise, Dijon, Worcestershire, bread crumbs, parsley, green onions, salt and pepper; mix well. Gently fold in crabmeat. Form into 3½-oz. cakes. Lightly dredge cakes in flour; shake off excess.

❷ In large skillet, heat oil over medium-high heat until hot. Add cakes; brown evenly on both sides. Serve with fresh lemon juice or sauce of your choice.

4 servings.

SHRIMP STEW

ALICE CHARLTON
MARATHON, FLORIDA

This was the first recipe I learned to cook, and it is still my favorite of mother's recipes.

¼	cup shortening
5	tablespoons all-purpose flour
⅓	cup chopped green onions
½	cup chopped celery
2	garlic cloves, minced
1	(8-oz.) can tomato sauce
3	cups water
1	teaspoon Worcestershire sauce
1½	teaspoons salt
½	teaspoon cayenne pepper
¼	teaspoon dry mustard
1	lb. shelled, deveined uncooked shrimp
4	cups hot cooked rice

❶ In large saucepan, melt shortening over medium-high heat. Add flour; stir constantly until mixture is smooth and golden brown. Add green onions, celery and garlic; cook until vegetables are tender. Reduce heat. Add tomato sauce, stirring carefully about 5 minutes. Add water, Worcestershire, salt, cayenne and mustard; simmer about 20 minutes. Add shrimp. Cover; simmer an additional 20 minutes more. Ladle into soup bowls over rice. Serve with garlic bread.

4 servings.

CHAMPAGNE TURKEY

PATRICIA McCUMBER
SEVIERVILLE, TENNESSEE

We love this recipe! You will too — just give it a try.

1   tablespoon salt
1   teaspoon celery salt
¾   teaspoon freshly ground pepper
1   (12-lb.) turkey
¼   cup butter or margarine
2   onions, sliced
2   tablespoons fresh parsley, finely chopped
½   teaspoon dried thyme
½   teaspoon dried marjoram
1   cup canned consommé
1   (750-ml) bottle Champagne
1   tablespoon all-purpose flour

❶ Heat oven to 425°F. In small bowl, combine salt, celery salt and pepper. Rub thoroughly into turkey, inside and out. Place turkey in large baking pan. Rub 3 tablespoons of the butter over breast and down sides. Bake 30 minutes.

❷ In medium bowl, stir together onions, parsley, thyme, marjoram and consommé. Pour over turkey. Reduce oven temperature to 325°F; continue baking 1 hour. Pour Champagne over turkey. Bake an additional 2 to 2½ hours or until internal temperature of inner thighs reaches 180°F. Basting frequently.

❸ Remove turkey to warmed platter; let stand in warm place 20 minutes. Strain pan gravy.

❹ In small saucepan, melt remaining tablespoon butter over medium heat. Stir in flour until smooth. Gradually add strained gravy. Stir; boil 5 minutes to thicken.

12 servings.

SUNDAY NIGHT TERRIFIC TUNABURGERS

GWEN CAMPBELL
STERLING, VIRGINIA

We enjoy these burgers every Sunday night as we gather around the kitchen table to catch up on the week's activities.

1   (6½-oz.) can tuna, drained, flaked
⅓   cup mayonnaise
2   tablespoons sour cream
1   teaspoon fresh lemon juice
1   egg, lightly beaten
¾   cup dry bread crumbs
½   cup finely chopped celery
¼   cup finely chopped onion
¼   cup finely chopped green, red or yellow bell pepper
½   cup vegetable oil
     Pickles and chips

❶ In medium bowl, stir together tuna, mayonnaise, sour cream, lemon juice, egg, bread crumbs, celery, onion and bell pepper. Cover and refrigerate 10 minutes. Shape mixture into 4 large or 8 small burgers.

❷ In large skillet, heat oil over medium-high heat until hot. Add burgers; cook, turning once, about 6 minutes or until golden brown on both sides. Serve burgers with pickles and chips on salad-size plates.

4 large or 8 small burgers.

SHRIMP WITH EVERYTHING

JOANNE BRYAN
ST. PETERSBURG, FLORIDA

The men in our family are excellent cooks. One of them shared this recipe with me.

1   tablespoon vegetable oil
1   lb. shelled, deveined uncooked small to medium shrimp
½   cup thinly sliced celery
1   small onion, chopped
1   small green or red bell pepper, cut into strips
1   (14½-oz.) can stewed tomatoes, undrained
1   (8-oz.) can tomato sauce
1   teaspoon hot pepper sauce or to taste
½   teaspoon garlic powder
½   teaspoon dried thyme
1½   cups instant rice

❶ In large skillet, heat oil over medium-high heat until hot. Add shrimp, celery, onion and bell pepper; cook until shrimp turn pink. Add tomatoes, tomato sauce, hot pepper sauce, garlic powder and thyme; bring to a boil. Stir in rice; cover. Remove from heat; let stand 10 minutes.

4 servings.

ROAST TURKEY WITH RICE STUFFING

SVETLANA DZHANGIROVA
SEATTLE, WASHINGTON

This recipe was passed down by my Armenian grandmother. She always served it during the holidays, especially Christmas.

1   cup long-grain rice
1   cup dried apricots, chopped
3   tablespoons golden raisins
6   tablespoons butter, softened
⅔   cup blanched slivered almonds
1   teaspoon ground cinnamon
½   teaspoon ground cloves
⅛   teaspoon salt
⅛   teaspoon freshly ground pepper
1   (8- to 10-lb.) frozen turkey, defrosted

❶ In medium saucepan, cook rice in boiling salted water until partially cooked; drain.

❷ Wash apricots and raisins in hot water. Drain liquid into large nonstick saucepan. In same saucepan, heat 3 tablespoons of the butter over medium heat. Add apricots, raisins and almonds. Sprinkle with cinnamon and cloves; stir over medium heat, about 5 minutes. Add rice; stir well to mix. Sauté 1 minute. Stir in salt and pepper. Set aside.

❸ Heat oven to 350°F. Twist turkey wing tips up and over; secure with string.

❹ Rub remaining 3 tablespoons butter over turkey. Sprinkle with salt and pepper; place breast-side up in large baking pan. Bake uncovered 3 to 3½ hours, basting occasionally, until internal temperature of inner thighs reaches 180°F. (If bird browns before it is cooked, cover with aluminum foil and continue baking.) Let bird stand, wrapped in foil, 20 minutes. If desired, thicken pan drippings for gravy.

❺ Place stuffing in oven. Cook until temperature reaches 165°F. Serve turkey with stuffing and gravy separately.

8 to 10 servings.

SEAFOOD LASAGNA

LARRAINE STETZEL
ALLENTOWN, PENNSYLVANIA

I first created this dish for a fancy buffet. It is great served with steamed asparagus.

2   tablespoons butter
1   tablespoon all-purpose flour
1   cup milk or half-and-half
½   cup Chardonnay
1   teaspoon paprika
2   green onions, sliced
2   cups crabmeat
1   cup (4 oz.) shredded cheddar cheese, plus more if needed
1   cup steamed jumbo shrimp, chopped
9   to 12 cooked lasagna noodles
3   grilled or broiled portobello mushroom caps, chopped

❶ In medium saucepan, melt butter over medium-high heat. Stir in flour over medium-low heat until well combined. Gradually add milk, whisking until lumps disappear. Heat, whisking frequently, until sauce is bubbly and slightly thickened. Stir in Chardonnay, paprika and green onions; continue cooking until heated through. Add crabmeat, cheddar and shrimp; stir until cheese melts. Heat oven to 400°F.

❷ To assemble lasagna: Spray 13x9-inch pan with nonstick cooking spray. Layer 3 or 4 of the noodles, half of the crab mixture and half of the mushrooms. Repeat once, reserving small amount of crab mixture. Top with remaining 3 or 4 noodles and remaining crab mixture. Sprinkle with additional cheddar, if desired. Bake, covered with aluminum foil, 30 minutes. Uncover and bake an additional 10 minutes. Cut into squares; serve warm.

6 to 8 servings.

SEAFOOD LASAGNA

CHICKEN BAKED IN SESAME

RUTH MILSTEIN
FOREST HILLS, NEW YORK

This recipe is my Israeli family's treasure with my own original inspiration.

1   egg
2   tablespoons soy sauce
1   cup bread crumbs
½   cup sesame seeds
½   teaspoon ground ginger
4   chicken legs, halved, boned and skinned
¼   cup margarine, melted
½   lemon, sliced

❶ Heat oven to 400°F.

❷ In medium bowl, beat egg and soy sauce. In another medium bowl, mix bread crumbs, sesame seeds and ginger. Dip and coat chicken legs in egg mixture, then coat with bread crumb mixture.

❸ Place chicken in 13x9-inch pan; drizzle with margarine. Bake 20 to 30 minutes or until internal temperature reaches 160°F, and chicken is no longer pink in center. Serve hot with lemon slices.

4 to 6 servings.

BAKED CHICKEN

WILLY WILKINS
RICHMOND HILL, ONTARIO, CANADA

I grew up in a large family, so the easier and faster the recipe, the better! This recipe is easy to prepare and truly delicious.

4   chicken legs
4   medium potatoes
1   large white onion, sliced
½   cup bread crumbs
¼   cup freshly grated Parmesan cheese
2   tablespoons chopped fresh parsley
2   to 3 teaspoons freshly ground pepper
1   teaspoon poultry seasoning
2   garlic cloves, minced
¼   cup water
¼   cup olive oil

❶ Heat oven to 325°F. In shallow baking pan, place chicken and potatoes in single layer; arrange sliced onion on top.

❷ In large bowl, combine bread crumbs, Parmesan, parsley, pepper, poultry seasoning and garlic; sprinkle over onion. Pour water and oil over entire dish. Bake covered 45 minutes. Uncover and bake an additional 30 minutes.

4 to 6 servings.

COUNTRY CAPTAIN

CAROL MERRILL
BERRIEN SPRINGS, MICHIGAN

This recipe has been in our family for four generations. It is traditionally passed on as part of the wedding gift from mother to daughter or mother-in-law to daughter-in-law.

1   (5-lb.) stewing chicken, cut into pieces
2   quarts water
2   bay leaves
2   ribs celery, cut into 2-inch pieces
1   medium onion, cut in half
4   teaspoons salt
2   tablespoons vegetable oil
2   large green bell peppers, diced
1   cup chopped onion
1   tablespoon curry powder
½   teaspoon dried thyme
     Dash cayenne pepper
2   garlic cloves, crushed
2   (28-oz.) cans whole tomatoes, undrained
2   (10-oz.) pkg. frozen okra
1   teaspoon sugar

❶ Place chicken in large saucepan. Add water, bay leaves, celery, medium onion and 2 teaspoons of the salt. Heat to a boil over high heat. Reduce heat; cover. Simmer 1½ to 2 hours or until tender. Remove chicken from pan with slotted spoon; cool. Strain stock, reserving 4 cups.

❷ In clean large saucepan, heat oil over medium-high heat. Add bell peppers, chopped onion, curry powder, thyme, cayenne and garlic; sauté 3 to 5 minutes or until tender. Add tomatoes, okra, sugar, remaining 2 teaspoons salt and reserved 4 cups stock. Simmer uncovered 35 minutes, stirring occasionally. Remove skin and bones from chicken; cut into bite-size pieces. Add to soup; simmer uncovered 15 minutes.

8 (1½-cup) servings.

CHICKEN SPEZZATINO

BARBARA BARTOLOMEO
RADNOR, PENNSYLVANIA

This is my husband's favorite chicken dish. I've been making it for many years. It's great for dinner or a buffet.

1 cup dry white wine
¼ cup brandy
2 garlic cloves, crushed
4 yellow bell peppers
¾ cup olive oil
1 (4-lb.) frying chicken, cut up
⅛ teaspoon salt
⅛ teaspoon freshly ground pepper
All-purpose flour for dusting
½ cup chopped onion
3 (14½-oz.) cans whole peeled tomatoes, drained
1 tablespoon fresh basil, chopped

❶ In small bowl, combine wine, brandy and garlic; let stand 1 hour.

❷ Roast bell peppers over open gas burner or under electric broiler until charred on each side, about 1 to 2 minutes. Peel off charred skin; remove seeds. Cut roasted peppers into strips.

❸ In large skillet, heat ¼ cup of the oil over medium-high heat. Add bell peppers; sauté about 10 minutes. Remove from heat; set aside.

❹ Season chicken with salt and pepper; dust with flour. In large saucepan, heat remaining ½ cup oil over medium-high heat. Add chicken; fry on both sides, a few pieces at a time. When pieces are fully cooked, transfer to hot serving platter to keep warm. Pour off all but 2 tablespoons of oil; sauté onion until golden. Stir in wine mixture; reduce by half over high heat. Add tomatoes and basil; season with salt and pepper. Simmer 15 minutes. Return chicken to skillet; simmer an additional 5 minutes. Arrange chicken on platter; top with sauce and roasted bell peppers.

4 to 6 servings.

CHICKEN IN A WINE CREAM SAUCE

MARTHA RAU
SALINAS, CALIFORNIA

My family enjoys this recipe immensely.

4 large chicken breasts
1 onion, cut up
1½ cups diced celery
6 black peppercorns
⅛ teaspoon salt
1 garlic clove, crushed
¼ cup butter
1 small onion, chopped
2 teaspoons paprika
2½ tablespoons all-purpose flour
1 cup dry white wine
½ cup sour cream
⅛ teaspoon freshly ground pepper
1 (14-oz.) can artichoke hearts, drained

❶ In large pot, bring chicken, cut-up onion, celery, peppercorns, salt, garlic and enough water to cover to a boil over medium-high heat. Cook 15 minutes or until chicken is no longer pink. Reserve 1 cup stock, discarding onion, celery, peppercorns and garlic.

❷ In medium saucepan, melt butter over medium-high heat; add onion and paprika; sauté until tender. Add flour; stir until combined. Remove from heat; gradually add reserved stock and wine. Return to heat; stir until sauce boils and thickens. Reduce heat; simmer 2 minutes. Stir in sour cream until combined. Remove from heat; season with salt and pepper to taste.

❸ Heat oven to 350°F. Remove bones and skin from chicken; cut into large dice.

❹ In Dutch oven, combine chicken and artichoke hearts; top with sauce. Cover; bake 20 minutes or until heated through. Serve with noodles and rice. Can be made a day ahead and frozen.

4 servings.

CHICKEN IN BRANDY ALFREDO

CAROLYN OLESEN
TECUMSEH, NEBRASKA

This was the first recipe I ever made for my husband. He went absolutely nuts for it! I always make it when I want to do something special just for him.

4   boneless skinless chicken breast halves,
     cut into bite-size pieces
½   cup plus 2 tablespoons olive oil
¼   cup dry white wine
2   garlic cloves, minced
1   tablespoon chopped fresh basil, or 1 teaspoon dried
¾   Cup freshly grated Parmesan cheese
2   cups broccoli florets
8   oz. fettuccine or other favorite pasta
¼   cup butter
8   oz. sliced mushrooms
½   cup brandy
1   cup heavy cream

❶ Place chicken in shallow bowl. In medium bowl, whisk together ½ cup of the oil, wine, garlic and basil; pour over chicken. Marinate chicken at least 1 hour.

❷ Heat large skillet over medium-high heat. With slotted spoon, lift chicken from marinade in skillet; stir-fry chicken, stirring constantly, until lightly browned. Remove from skillet; drain on paper towels. Sprinkle with ¼ cup of the Parmesan while still hot. Discard marinade.

❸ Add remaining 2 tablespoons oil to skillet. Stir-fry broccoli 5 to 7 minutes or until just crisp-tender. Remove from pan; set on top of chicken on paper towels. Sprinkle with Parmesan. (You can do this up to a day in advance. Cover and chill; bring to room temperature before continuing with recipe.)

❹ Cook pasta according to package directions. Rinse; drain. Set aside.

❺ Meanwhile, reduce heat to medium. In clean large skillet, melt butter. Add mushrooms; sauté 5 minutes or until cooked. Remove from heat. Add brandy; flame, shaking pan until flames subside. Return to heat, increasing to medium-high. Stir in cream. When cream starts to simmer, return chicken and broccoli to pan. Begin adding remaining ½ cup Parmesan, a little at a time. Stir and simmer 10 minutes or until sauce thickens. Add pasta, a little at a time; stir until well mixed. Divide among 4 serving bowls; garnish with additional Parmesan.

4 servings.

APRICOT MUSTARD CHICKEN BREASTS

DAVID RITTER
DOUGLASSVILLE, PENNSYLVANIA

We like to serve healthy portions for guests. My wife came up with this very simple preparation for chicken; it requires very little prep time, but doesn't sacrifice flavor.

⅔   cup water
¼   cup Dijon mustard
6   tablespoons apricot preserves
1   tablespoon soy sauce
1   tablespoon finely chopped green onion
4   boneless skinless chicken breast halves

❶ In large nonstick skillet, stir together water, Dijon, preserves, soy sauce and green onion. Add chicken; bring to a simmer over medium-high heat. Reduce heat; gently simmer, covered, 15 to 18 minutes or until chicken is tender. (If sauce becomes too thick, add more water while cooking.)

4 servings.

KYLIE'S SHEPHERD'S PIE

KYLIE CHUNTZ
HAWTHORNE, CALIFORNIA

This is a south-of-the-border spin on the traditional Shepherd's Pie *my mother made for us while growing up in Australia. My sister and I experimented with different seasonings over the years until we decided this was a keeper.*

½   cup olive oil
1   onion, chopped
1   green bell pepper, chopped
⅛   teaspoon salt
⅛   teaspoon freshly ground pepper
1½ lb. ground turkey
1   teaspoon minced garlic
2   carrots, chopped
1   (1.5-oz.) pkg. taco seasoning
1   cup peas, frozen or fresh
1   (14.5-oz.) can tomatoes
    Ground cumin and chili powder to taste (optional)
2   lb. russet potatoes, peeled, cooked and mashed
    (I always add a little milk and butter to potatoes
    when mashing.)
1   cup grated cheddar cheese

❶ Heat oven to 350°F. In large saucepan, heat oil over medium-high heat until hot. Add onion and bell pepper; sauté until tender. Season with salt and pepper. Add turkey and garlic; cook until turkey is no longer pink. Add carrots and taco seasoning; cook 3 to 4 minutes. Add peas and tomatoes; simmer 10 minutes. Taste; adjust seasoning with cumin and chili powder, if using.

❷ Pour turkey mixture into 3-quart casserole; top with mashed potatoes, smoothing evenly to cover entire surface. Sprinkle with cheese. Bake 45 minutes or until cheese is slightly brown and bubbling.

4 to 6 servings.

CHICKEN CURRY

ETHELYN WELLES
BELLA VISTA, ARKANSAS

This recipe has been a family favorite since childhood.

CURRY
2   tablespoons butter, melted
1¼ teaspoons mild curry powder
2   tablespoons all-purpose flour
2   cups diced cooked chicken or turkey
1   garlic clove, minced
1   cup reduced-sodium chicken broth
1   cup milk

CHUTNEY
1   cup white vinegar
¾   cup packed brown sugar
1   teaspoon celery salt
¼   teaspoon freshly ground pepper
¼   teaspoon ground ginger
4   to 5 apples, chopped
3   small onions, chopped
1   garlic clove, finely chopped
½   cup raisins

❶ For Curry: In medium saucepan, melt butter over medium-high heat. Stir in curry powder. Stir in flour. (It is important to combine butter and curry powder before adding flour.) Add turkey, garlic, broth and milk; simmer about 15 minutes. Refrigerate 1 to 2 hours to enhance flavors. Reheat to serve.

❷ For Chutney: In large saucepan, combine vinegar, brown sugar, celery salt, pepper, ginger, apples, onions, garlic and raisins. Simmer, stirring occasionally, about 30 minutes or until slightly thickened.

4 servings.

APPLE-STUFFED PORK LOIN

APPLE-STUFFED PORK LOIN

TRICIA CARPENTER
CORINTH, NEW YORK

This recipe was given to me by a friend. I like to make it on special occasions.

PORK
1½ lb. boneless pork loin
1 teaspoon salt
 Dash ground ginger
 Dash ground cloves

FILLING
2 green onions, finely chopped
2 green apples, grated or finely chopped
2 tablespoons butter, softened
2 tablespoons packed brown sugar
1 tablespoon prepared mustard

GARNISH
Sautéed apple slices or wedges

❶ Heat oven to 350°F. For Pork: With sharp knife, make slits across loin, deep enough to hold filling, but not all the way through.

❷ For Filling: In large bowl, stir together onions, apples, butter, brown sugar and mustard; set aside.

❸ Rub salt, ginger and cloves all over pork loin; place pork in 3-quart casserole.. Spoon filling into slits on loin. Place remaining filling around pork. Bake 1¼ to 1½ hours or until juices run clear. Let pork stand, covered with aluminum foil, at least 15 minutes before carving.

❹ When ready to serve, slice and spoon pan juices over pork. Surround with filling. Garnish with sautéed apples.

6 servings.

CROWN ROAST OF PORK

CAROL HAWLEY
FREDERICK, MARYLAND

I've been making this recipe for 25 years and it has always been my favorite. If Christmas or Easter is at my house, my guests can count on this!

8 oz. bulk pork sausage
2 tablespoons finely chopped onion
1 small garlic clove, minced
4 cups firm-textured bread cubes (5½ slices)
1½ cups cranberries, chopped
1 cup chopped walnuts
¼ teaspoon dried sage, crushed
¾ to 1 cup reduced-sodium chicken broth
1 (7- to 7½-lb.) pork rib crown roast (14 to 16 ribs)
⅛ teaspoon salt
⅛ teaspoon freshly ground pepper

❶ Heat oven to 325°F.

❷ In large saucepan or Dutch oven, cook sausage, onion and garlic over medium-high heat until meat is brown and onion in tender. Stir in bread cubes, cranberries, walnuts and sage. Add enough broth to moisten; toss gently to mix.

❸ Season crown roast with salt and pepper. Place roast, bone-side up, on aluminum foil on rack in shallow baking pan. Spoon about 3 cups sausage stuffing into center of roast. Insert meat thermometer into thickest portion of pork, away from fat or bone. Cover top loosely with aluminium foil. Bake 3½ to 4 hours or until thermometer reads 170°F.

❹ Spoon remaining stuffing into 1-quart casserole. Bake covered during final 30 to 45 minutes of pork baking time. Uncover stuffed roast during last 15 minutes. If desired, place paper ruffles on rib bones. Let stand 15 minutes before carving.

14 to 16 servings.

BRISKET OF BEEF

BEVERLEE SCHENKMAN
VERNON, NEW JERSEY

This is my Grandma Helen's recipe. She used to serve it on Rosh Hashanah.

1   to 2 tablespoons vegetable oil
1   (6- to 7-lb.) breast of beef or breast deckel
       (available only from Kosher butcher), well
          trimmed (beef brisket)
⅛   teaspoon garlic powder
⅛   teaspoon onion powder
⅛   teaspoon freshly ground pepper
4   large onions, sliced
3   large garlic cloves
1   cup water
1   cup ketchup
2   tablespoons Worcestershire sauce
1   envelope dry onion soup mix
⅛   teaspoon salt

❶ In large skillet, heat oil over medium-high heat until hot. Flavor meat with garlic powder, onion powder and pepper. Add beef to skillet; sear on both sides. Remove beef from skillet. Add onions and garlic; reduce heat. Add water; scrape bottom of skillet to loosen browned bits. Stir in ketchup, Worcestershire and soup mix. Gravy should be thick. Return beef to skillet. Cover; simmer over low heat about 2½ hours, turning once during cooking. Beef should be fork-tender. Cool; slice. Return beef to gravy and serve.

14 to 16 servings.

GRANDMA'S SAUERBRATEN

HARRY CHRISTIANSON
KISSIMMEE, FLORIDA

As a child, I went to Grandma's house every Christmas. We looked forward to this recipe because it was so good and because no one else could replicate it.

1   (3- to 4-lb.) beef bottom round
1   teaspoon salt
½   teaspoon freshly ground pepper
2   medium onions, thinly sliced
1   carrot, sliced
1   rib celery, chopped
4   whole cloves
4   black peppercorns
2   cups red wine vinegar
2   bay leaves
4   cups water
2   tablespoons olive oil
6   tablespoons butter
5   tablespoons all-purpose flour
1   tablespoon sugar
15   gingersnaps, crushed

❶ Sprinkle beef with salt and pepper; place in glass or stainless steel bowl. In large bowl, combine onions, carrot, celery, cloves, peppercorns, vinegar, bay leaves and 4 cups water; remove and reserve 3 cups. Add beef to bowl; cover and refrigerate up to 2 days. Remove beef from marinade; discard marinade.

❷ In Dutch oven, heat oil and 1 tablespoon of the butter over medium-low heat. Add beef. Increase heat to medium-high. Brown beef on all sides. Add reserved marinade and all of its vegetables. Bring to a boil; reduce heat to low. Cook 3 hours.

❸ In small saucepan, melt remaining 5 tablespoons butter over medium heat. Whisk in flour and sugar. Cook, stirring frequently, 6 to 8 minutes or until mixture just starts to brown. Blend into hot marinade mixture. Cover; cook 1 hour or until beef is fork-tender. Remove bay leaves. Remove beef from Dutch oven; keep warm. Stir in gingersnaps; stir constantly until thickened. Serve gravy over beef. Serve with potato dumplings and red cabbage.

6 to 8 servings.

ROY'S FAVORITE POT ROAST

MABLE WATSON
LENDIR, NORTH CAROLINA

This 50-year-old recipe is a favorite in our house.

¼   cup shortening
1   (4- to 4½-lb.) pot roast
1½ tablespoons packed brown sugar
1   tablespoon dry mustard
1   tablespoon salt
¼   teaspoon freshly ground pepper
¼   cup vinegar
¼   cup water

❶ In Dutch oven, melt shortening over medium-high heat. Add roast; slowly brown roast on all sides.

❷ In small bowl, mix together brown sugar, mustard, salt and pepper; sprinkle over top of roast. Add vinegar and water. Cover; gently simmer 4 hours or until tender. Thicken gravy, if desired, just before serving.

8 servings.

GLAZED CORNED BEEF

NANCY WALKER
WOOD RIVER, ILLINOIS

This is my grandmother's recipe and a family favorite.

3   cups corned beef
1   cup orange marmalade
¼   cup Dijon mustard
¼   cup packed brown sugar

❶ In large pot, cover corned beef with boiling water; bring to a boil over medium-high heat. Reduce heat; cover partially. Simmer as slowly as possible 3 hours or until beef is fork-tender. Remove beef from pot; drain.

❷ Heat oven to 350°F. In small bowl, stir together marmalade, Dijon and brown sugar. Place beef in baking dish; pour marmalade mixture over, coating beef thoroughly. Bake 30 minutes or until glaze is crisp and brown. Serve hot or at room temperature.

8 servings.

BARBECUED SPARERIBS

DIANE CUPPLES
BUFFALO, NEW YORK

My father loved spareribs and homegrown vegetables in the summertime. He's passed on now, but my brother and I still enjoy his recipe.

2   lb. spareribs (cut into pieces for serving)
¼   cup chopped onion
1   tablespoon bacon fat
1   cup chili sauce
⅔   cup water
2   tablespoons vinegar
¼   cup lemon juice
2   tablespoons packed brown sugar
¼   teaspoon salt
¼   teaspoon paprika

❶ Heat oven to 500°F. Place spareribs in 3-quart casserole; cover with parchment paper. Bake 15 minutes. Reduce oven temperature to 350°F.

❷ Meanwhile, in medium skillet, sauté onion in bacon fat over medium-high heat until brown. Stir in chili sauce, water, vinegar, lemon juice, brown sugar, salt and paprika.

❸ Remove parchment paper from ribs. Pour sauce over spareribs; bake 1½ hours.

4 servings.

AUNT ROSIE'S MEATBALLS

BRENDA ARMENTROUT
KANSAS CITY, KANSAS

My aunt makes these meatballs every Fourth of July. They are fantastic!

MEATBALLS
3   lb. ground beef
2   cups quick cooking oats
1   cup chopped onion
1   (12-oz.) can evaporated milk
2   eggs, beaten
2   teaspoons salt
2   teaspoons chili powder
½   teaspoon garlic powder
½   teaspoon freshly ground pepper

SAUCE
4   cups ketchup or tomato sauce
3   tablespoons liquid smoke
3   cups packed brown sugar
1   cup chopped onion
1   teaspoon garlic powder

❶ Heat oven to 350°F.

❷ For Meatballs: In large bowl, mix together beef, oats, 1 cup onion, evaporated milk, eggs, salt, chili powder, ½ teaspoon garlic powder and pepper. Shape into 1-inch meatballs.

❸ For Sauce: In clean large bowl, stir together ketchup, liquid smoke, brown sugar, 1 cup onion and 1 teaspoon garlic powder; pour over meatballs. Bake 1 hour or until meatballs are done.

10 to 12 servings.

THE ULTIMATE LONDON BROIL

PEGGY POINTER
KETTERING, OHIO

This is my all-time favorite recipe and I rarely share it. The recipe was given to me several years ago by a cook I greatly admire, James Beard. Here's my adaptation.

Unseasoned meat tenderizer (optional)
1   (3- to 3½-lb.) top round
½   cup vegetable oil
½   cup Burgundy wine
¼   cup soy sauce
2   tablespoons ketchup
1   tablespoon curry powder
1   tablespoon ground ginger
½   teaspoon freshly ground pepper
2   garlic cloves, sliced

❶ If using tenderizer, moisten surface of steak. Sprinkle liberally with tenderizer; prick entire surface with fork. Set aside.

❷ In 13x9-inch pan, combine oil, wine, soy sauce, ketchup, curry powder, ginger, pepper and garlic; mix well. Place meat in pan, turning to coat. Cover; refrigerate 24 hours, turning once or twice.

❸ Remove steak from marinade; discard marinade. Grill to desired doneness. Slice diagonally into thin slices.

8 to 10 servings.

BURGUNDIAN BEEF

HERB NASH
LITHONIA, GEORGIA

I inherited this simple recipe from my grandmother. It has served me and my family well.

1	tablespoon butter
¼	lb. salt pork, diced
3	lb. beef rump or sirloin tip, cut into 1-inch cubes
3	cups minced onions
1	carrot, sliced
2	small shallots, minced
1	garlic clove, minced
2	cups Burgundy wine
1	tablespoon tarragon vinegar or white vinegar
2	tablespoons minced fresh parsley
2	tablespoons minced fresh chervil
⅛	teaspoon dried thyme
6	peppercorns
2	bay leaves
	Salt to taste

❶ In large saucepan, melt butter over medium-high heat. Add pork; sauté 2 to 3 minutes. Add beef; sear thoroughly in hot fat. Remove beef; set aside. Add onions, carrot, shallots and garlic to saucepan; simmer until onions are light yellow. Stir in beef, Burgundy, vinegar, parsley, chervil, thyme, peppercorns, bay leaves and salt. Cook over very low heat 3 hours. Remove bay leaves. Serve with or over rice.

8 servings.

TURKEY MEATBALLS IN TANGY CRANBERRY SAUCE

BARBARA NOWAKOWSKI
NORTH TONAWANDA, NEW YORK

These turkey meatballs and their sauce burst with flavor.

1	lb. ground turkey
½	cup dry bread crumbs
½	teaspoon salt
¼	teaspoon freshly ground pepper
¼	cup milk
½	teaspoon plus 1 tablespoon Worcestershire sauce
1	small onion, chopped (¼ cup)
1	egg
1	tablespoon vegetable oil
1	(8-oz.) can whole-berry cranberry sauce
1	(8-oz.) can tomato sauce
2	tablespoons prepared horseradish
1	tablespoon lemon juice

❶ In large bowl, mix together turkey, bread crumbs, salt, pepper, milk, ½ teaspoon Worcestershire, onion and egg. Shape mixture into 20 (1½-inch) balls. For cocktail meatballs, shape mixture into 1-inch meatballs.

❷ In medium skillet, heat oil over medium heat. Cook meatballs in oil, turning occasionally, 10 minutes or until brown. Stir in cranberry sauce, tomato sauce, horseradish and lemon juice; heat to boiling. Reduce heat; simmer uncovered, stirring occasionally, about 10 minutes or until meatballs are no longer pink in center.

36 meatballs.

RE-CREATED MEAT LOAF

MEANDY BISHOP
PECOS, NEW MEXICO

I love to experiment with recipes and I created this one from three or four different meat loaf versions. I'm told it's absolutely terrific.

MEATLOAF
1½ lb. ground beef
1   egg, beaten
1   cup bread crumbs
1   tablespoon minced onion
¼   cup shredded carrot
2½   tablespoons chopped fresh parsley
½   teaspoon dried thyme or oregano
½   teaspoon salt
¼   teaspoon freshly ground pepper
1½   cups (6 oz.) shredded mozzarella cheese
2   (8-oz.) cans tomato sauce

SAUCE
½   cup granulated sugar
2   tablespoons packed brown sugar
2   tablespoons vinegar
2   teaspoons prepared mustard

❶ Heat oven to 350°F. For Meatloaf: In medium bowl, mix together beef, egg, bread crumbs, onion, carrot, parsley, thyme, salt, pepper, mozzarella and 1 can of the tomato sauce. Spread mixture in 13x9-inch pan. Bake 50 minutes.

❷ Meanwhile, prepare Sauce: In small saucepan, combine remaining can of tomato sauce, granulated and brown sugars, vinegar and mustard. Bring to a boil over medium-high heat, stirring occasionally. Pour over meat loaf; bake 10 minutes. Cool 3 to 5 minutes before serving.

6 servings.

CHICKEN CACCIATORE

MARY KIRKLAND
LAS VEGAS, NEVADA

My mom taught me how to make this dish, but I've modified it over the years. My family loves it.

6   boneless skinless chicken breasts
1   cup chopped onion
1   green bell pepper, chopped
2   carrots, chopped
1   cup mushrooms, sliced
1   cup sliced ripe olives
⅛   teaspoon salt
⅛   teaspoon freshly ground pepper
½   cup chopped fresh cilantro
3   tablespoons canned diced green chiles
2   large ripe tomatoes, chopped
½   teaspoon dried oregano
½   teaspoon dried thyme
½   teaspoon minced garlic
5   tablespoons lime juice
1   (28-oz.) can stewed tomatoes, chopped

❶ Heat oven to 350°F. Place chicken breasts in 3-quart casserole. Add onion, bell pepper, carrots, mushrooms, olives, salt and pepper.

❷ In large bowl, mix together cilantro, chiles, ripe tomatoes, oregano, thyme, garlic, lime juice and stewed tomatoes. Pour over chicken. Cover with aluminum foil; bake 1 hour or until chicken is no longer pink in center.

6 servings.

CHICKEN CACCIATORE

INDIVIDUAL MEAT LOAF WELLINGTON

CHARLOTTE WARD
HILTON HEAD ISLAND, SOUTH CAROLINA

Two of my husband's favorite foods are meat loaf and Beef Wellington. One day I decided to combine both and came up with this — the star of my collection.

MEATLOAF
½ lb. ground beef
½ lb. ground veal
½ lb. ground pork
2 cups bread cubes, preferably mixture of white, whole wheat and rye
¾ cup milk
1 tablespoon Worcestershire sauce
1 egg, beaten
¼ cup minced onion
1¼ teaspoons salt
¼ teaspoon each: freshly ground pepper, dry mustard, dried thyme, crushed rosemary, dried sage, celery salt and garlic salt
3 tablespoons ketchup
2 cans liver pâté
1 pkg. frozen puff pastry, thawed
1 egg yolk, beaten

MADEIRA-BRANDY SAUCE
¼ cup butter
5 tablespoons all-purpose flour
2 cups beef consommé
1 tablespoon tomato paste
¼ teaspoon each: salt, crushed rosemary, dried thyme
Dash ground cloves
Dash freshly ground pepper
¼ teaspoon beef base
½ cup Madeira wine
1 tablespoon brandy
1 (7-oz.) pkg. frozen mushrooms, thawed

❶ Heat oven to 350°F. Line broiler pan and rack with aluminum foil. Spray foil with cooking spray; pierce foil to allow juices to drain.

❷ For Meatloaf: In large bowl, mix together beef, veal and pork. Mix in bread cubes. In small bowl, whisk together milk, Worcestershire and egg; add to meat mixture. In clean bowl, combine onion, salt, pepper, mustard, thyme, rosemary, sage, celery salt and garlic salt; mix into meat mixture. Form into 8 miniature loaves, about 3x2x1 inches each; place on pan. Bake 1 hour or until meat thermometer inserted in loaf reads 145°F.

❸ Cool loaves completely in refrigerator, about 1 hour. Remove from refrigerator; cover top of each loaf with thin layer of ketchup, then pâté.

❹ Heat oven to 425°F. Roll 1 sheet of puff pastry at a time to about ⅛ inch thick. Cut into fourths. Wrap each loaf in ¼ sheet of pastry (cut away excess pastry; set aside scraps to decorate loaves or for another purpose). Pierce top and sides gently with fork; brush with egg yolk. Refrigerate at least 2 hours. Bake 30 minutes or until thermometer reads 160°F.

❺ Meanwhile, prepare Sauce: In large saucepan, melt butter; whisk in flour. When smooth, stir in consommé, tomato paste, salt, rosemary, thyme, cloves, pepper and beef base. Bring to a boil. Continue stirring 2 to 3 minutes or until thickened. Slowly add wine, brandy and mushrooms. Serve over loaves.

8 servings.

MOM'S BARBECUED HAMBURGERS

KATELYNN WILCHER
MOORESVILLE, INDIANA

I learned a lot about cooking from my mom, a self-taught cook who loved to try new recipes. These burgers are so good you don't even need toppings.

1½ lb. ground beef chuck
1 red or white onion, chopped
1 teaspoon salt
½ teaspoon freshly ground pepper
½ cup cracker meal
½ cup Barbecue Sauce, plus more for basting

BARBECUE SAUCE
2 cups chili sauce
2 tablespoons Worcestershire sauce
2 teaspoons lemon juice
 Dash hot pepper sauce
¼ cup butter
1 teaspoon dry mustard
½ teaspoon garlic powder
½ teaspoon chili powder
1 small onion, chopped
2 bay leaves

❶ Heat grill. In bowl, combine beef, onion, salt, pepper, cracker meal and barbecue sauce; mix well. Shape into 8 burgers. Grill about 20 minutes, basting frequently with sauce. Near end of grilling time, brush cut sides of buns with sauce; toast cut-side down on grill.

❷ For Sauce: In large saucepan, combine chili sauce, Worcestershire, lemon juice, hot pepper sauce, butter, mustard, garlic powder, chili powder, onion and bay leaves; simmer 15 minutes. Remove bay leaves. Serve burgers on toasted hamburger buns.

8 burgers.

PORK CUTLETS ITALIANO

LINDA MANIA
OCALA, FLORIDA

This recipe is fabulous, and a favorite in my house.

1 lb. pork cutlets, thinly sliced
2 eggs, beaten
1½ cups dry Italian bread crumbs
½ cup olive oil
4 garlic cloves, sliced
1 cup white wine
½ cup Kalamata olives
½ cup sliced mushrooms (optional)
1 tablespoon fresh basil, chopped
1 teaspoon dried oregano
 Salt and freshly ground pepper to taste
1 tablespoon arrowroot powder

❶ Dip cutlets in eggs, then bread crumbs.

❷ In large saucepan, heat 7 tablespoons of the oil over medium-high heat. Add cutlets; brown. Set aside. Drain fat from saucepan. Add remaining tablespoon oil to saucepan; brown garlic. Stir in wine, olives, mushrooms, if using, basil, oregano, salt, pepper and arrowroot. Heat until mixture comes to a rolling boil; add cutlets. Reduce heat; simmer until sauce thickens. Serve with wide noodles or Italian bread.

4 servings.

CHRISTMAS MEAT PIE

LEESAN TRUMBLY
GRANT'S PASS, OREGON

I've made this recipe for years. It is a family tradition to have Christmas Meat Pie *at least once between December 16th and 25th.*

1   (3-lb.) chicken
3   lb. round steak
6   tablespoons butter
1   cup finely chopped celery
½   cup finely chopped onion
½   cup chopped fresh parsley
6   tablespoons all-purpose flour
2   teaspoons salt
1   teaspoon ground savory
½   teaspoon ground nutmeg
½   teaspoon dried thyme
½   teaspoon freshly ground pepper
¼   teaspoon ground cloves
2   (9-inch) unbaked double-crust pastries

❶ In 4-quart Dutch oven, cover chicken and steak with water. Cook 2 hours or until chicken is ready to fall off bone. Remove chicken and steak; reserve 3 cups stock, adding water if needed. Dice chicken and steak.

❷ Heat oven to 375°F. In large skillet, melt butter over medium-high heat. Add celery, onion and parsley; sauté until tender. In small bowl, mix together flour, salt, savory, nutmeg, thyme, pepper and cloves; stir into skillet. Stir in reserved stock. Cook over medium heat, stirring occasionally, until mixture thickens and bubbles. Pour into very large dish, stirring to mix.

❸ Roll out crusts for deep-dish pie plates. Line 2 pie plates with bottom crusts; fill with filling. Top with remaining crusts; crimp to seal edges. Bake 1 hour. Serve with mashed potatoes.

12 servings.

AWESOME CHILI DOG PIE

GWEN CAMPBELL
STERLING, VIRGINIA

My son was a boy scout, and we enjoyed having his entire troop over for a laughter- and fun-filled time at our house. This dish was always requested.

2½ cups buttermilk baking mix
6   tablespoons water
1   tablespoon prepared mustard
2   (16-oz.) pkg. beef or pork hot dogs
2   (15-oz.) cans chili, with or without beans
1   cup (4 oz.) shredded cheddar cheese
    Potato or nacho chips, crumbled

❶ Heat oven to 350°F. Spray 13x9-inch pan with nonstick cooking spray.

❷ In small bowl, combine baking mix, water and mustard; stir until dough forms. With fingertips dipped in baking mix, press dough into bottom and up sides of pan; set aside.

❸ Quarter hot dogs by cutting in half lengthwise and again crosswise. Place hot dogs on dough; spoon chili over hot dogs. Sprinkle with cheddar and potato chips. Bake 30 minutes or until crust is golden and pie is heated through.

8 servings.

PIZZA RUSTICA

ROSE DeVITO
LONG BRANCH, NEW JERSEY

This recipe for a stuffed Italian Pie is an Italian Easter tradition brought to America almost 47 years ago by my mother. She makes it every year and it's everyone's favorite dish. You eat it for the first time the day after Good Friday (Holy Saturday) and then again on Easter.

CRUST
1½ tablespoons active dry yeast
1 tablespoon sugar
1¼ cups warm water (105°F to 115°F)
4 cups all-purpose flour
2 eggs, beaten
¼ cup margarine or butter, softened
½ teaspoon salt

FILLING
1 lb. Soppressata
10 eggs
2 lb. basket cheese (available at Italian delis
    or specialty stores)
1 cup freshly grated Parmesan cheese

❶ Heat oven to 375°F. Spray 13x9-inch pan with nonstick cooking spray.

❷ For Crust: in small bowl, dissolve yeast and sugar in warm water; let sit about 5 minutes. Place flour in large bowl; make a well in center of flour. Add yeast mixture, beaten eggs, margarine and salt. With fingers, slowly start adding flour from the inside out until all flour is gone and you have formed a ball. Knead about 10 minutes on lightly floured surface. If dough is too stiff, add a little water; if too sticky, add a little flour. Place dough in large greased bowl; let rise in warm place, away from drafts, 3 hours. Split dough into 2 balls; let each rise separately 1 hour.

❸ Meanwhile, prepare Filling: Slice Soppressata into ¼-inch slices; cut each slice into 4 pieces. In large bowl, beat 10 eggs. Add basket cheese, Soppressata and Parmesan; mix well.

❹ Heat oven to 375°F. Roll 1 of the dough balls into rectangle large enough to fit in bottom and up sides of pan. Line pan with dough; pour in filling. Roll remaining ball to fit over top of pan, overlapping a little. Pinch crusts together to seal. With fork, pierce holes in top crust. Bake 1 hour or until crust is golden brown.

8 servings.

HUNGARIAN GOULASH

LEANNE LEASURE
SUMNER, IOWA

This was the dish my father was requested to make for each of his five kids' birthdays while we grew up. We never tired of it.

1 cup chopped onion
1 garlic clove, minced
2 tablespoons all-purpose flour
1 teaspoon salt
½ teaspoon freshly ground pepper
½ teaspoon paprika
¼ teaspoon dried thyme, crushed
1 bay leaf
1 (14½-oz.) can whole tomatoes, sliced
2 lb. round steak
1 cup sour cream

❶ In crockpot, mix onion, garlic, flour, salt, pepper, paprika, thyme, bay leaf and tomatoes. Add round steak; stir to coat. Cook on Low 8 to 10 hours or High 4 to 5 hours. Thirty minutes before serving, remove bay leaf; stir in sour cream. Serve over hot noodles or rice.

8 servings.

PERSONAL SAUSAGE MEAT LOAF

DAVID RITTER
DOUGLASSVILLE, PENNSYLVANIA

Our lunch and dinner guests enjoy a personal serving of meat loaf along with traditional mashed potatoes. Italian sausage adds a unique flavor, and the bread crumbs and liquid help make each loaf tender and moist.

MEATLOAF
½ cup olive oil
½ cup chopped onion
2 garlic cloves, chopped
1 lb. bulk Italian sausage
½ cup bread crumbs
1 egg
½ cup water
3 tablespoons light cream

SAUCE
3 tablespoons water
2 tablespoons ketchup
1 tablespoon barbecue sauce

❶ For Meatloaf: In large skillet, heat oil over medium-high heat. Add onion and garlic; sauté until onion is transparent, being careful not to burn garlic. Remove from heat; cool.

❷ In large bowl, combine sausage and cooled onion mixture; mix well (clean hands work well for mixing). Add ¼ cup of the bread crumbs; mix well. Add egg; mix well. Mix in ¼ cup of the water. Add remaining ¼ cup bread crumbs; mix again. Mix in cream and remaining ¼ cup water until uniform. (Mixture will be soft, but firm enough to maintain its shape when formed into loaf.)

❸ Heat oven to 350°F. Spray 1-quart casserole with nonstick cooking spray. Form sausage mixture into 4 miniature loaves. Place in casserole, being careful loaves do not touch.

❹ For Sauce: In small bowl, stir together water, ketchup and barbecue sauce. Spread over each loaf. Bake about 25 minutes. Cover; continue baking about 10 minutes. (If loaves are not covered during last part of baking, they may dry out.) Remove from oven; cool 5 minutes before serving. Meat loaves should be moist in center and not overdone.

4 servings.

HOT CHICKEN SALAD

MARTHE MILLER
JACKSONVILLE, NORTH CAROLINA

My mother always makes this recipe for church get-togethers; everyone always raves about its great flavor.

3 cups diced cooked chicken
1 cup chopped celery
1 cup cooked long-grain white rice
½ cup chopped green bell pepper
3 hard-cooked eggs, chopped
1 (8-oz.) can sliced water chestnuts, drained
1 (4-oz.) can mushroom stems and pieces, drained
1 (2-oz.) jar diced pimientos, drained
¾ cup mayonnaise
1 teaspoon lemon juice
1 (10¾-oz.) can cream of chicken soup
¼ cup butter, melted
1 cup corn flakes, crushed
½ cup sliced almonds

❶ Heat oven to 350°F. Spray 13x9-inch pan with nonstick cooking spray.

❷ In large bowl, mix together chicken, celery, rice, bell pepper, eggs, water chestnuts, mushrooms, pimientos, mayonnaise, lemon juice and soup. Spread into pan.

❸ In small bowl, mix together butter, corn flakes and almonds; sprinkle over chicken mixture. Bake uncovered 45 minutes.

8 servings.

SIDES

MASHED POTATO CASSEROLE

JANYA PEGRAM
BETHANY, OKLAHOMA

*It would not be a holiday if our aunt did not bring this dish.
We'd never see her, because nobody would let her in without it!*

5   lb. potatoes, cooked, mashed
2   (3-oz.) pkg. cream cheese
1   cup sour cream
¾   cup butter
⅓   cup chopped green onions
1   teaspoon salt
⅛   teaspoon freshly ground pepper
    Crushed butter crackers

❶ Heat oven to 350°F. Spray 3-quart casserole with
nonstick cooking spray.

❷ In large bowl, combine potatoes, cream cheese,
sour cream, ¼ cup of the butter, green onions, salt
and pepper; mix well. Spread mixture into bottom
of casserole; dot with remaining ½ cup butter.
Sprinkle crackers around edge. Bake uncovered 30
minutes. Store in refrigerator up to 2 days.

10 servings.

TURKISH BEANS

JENNIFER OKUTMAN
WESTMINSTER, MARYLAND

*This is my mother-in-law's recipe. (My father-in-law is
Turkish.) It makes a great side dish for any meal.*

3   to 4 tablespoons olive oil
1   medium onion, thinly sliced
1   lb. fresh green beans, trimmed
3   medium tomatoes, sliced
3   tablespoons sugar
⅛   teaspoon salt
⅛   teaspoon freshly ground pepper
¼   cup plain yogurt, for drizzling (optional)

❶ In large skillet, heat oil over medium-high heat
until hot. Add onion, beans, tomatoes, sugar, salt
and pepper; sauté 3 to 4 minutes. Cover; cook 25
to 30 minutes, or until beans are tender. Serve hot
or cold. Drizzle with yogurt, if desired.

6 servings.

OVEN FRIES

KYLIE CHUNTZ
HAWTHORNE, CALIFORNIA

*This recipe can be adapted to use russet, sweet or butternut
potatoes. A combination of all three is quite delicious too.*

1   lb. potatoes, peeled
    Olive oil, for coating
⅛   teaspoon salt
⅛   teaspoon freshly ground pepper
¼   teaspoon chili powder

❶ Heat oven to 450°F. Cut potatoes in half lengthwise,
then into thirds lengthwise; arrange in 13x9-inch
pan. Pour enough oil over potatoes to coat; toss.
Season with salt, pepper and chili powder. Bake 20
minutes or until browned on the bottom. Turn; bake
20 to 30 minutes more or until potatoes are evenly
golden brown. Serve immediately.

4 servings.

POTATO PANCAKES

AMY COX
COMMACK, NEW YORK

*This is my grandfather's recipe, which has been made by my
family every holiday, especially Passover. It has become even
more meaningful since his passing in 2000.*

4   medium potatoes, peeled, grated
1   medium onion, grated, juice reserved
1   egg
1   tablespoon all-purpose flour
½   teaspoon salt
½   teaspoon freshly ground pepper
¼   cup vegetable oil

❶ In large bowl, combine potatoes, onion, reserved
onion juice, egg and flour; mix well. Add salt and
pepper.

❷ In large skillet, heat oil over medium-high heat
until hot. Add tablespoonfuls of the potato
mixture; cook until edges brown. Turn over; cook
an additional 2 minutes.

4 servings.

SWEET POTATO SOUFFLE

PEGGY POINTER
KETTERING, OHIO

This wonderfully different sweet potato dish is a delicious change from the traditional candied treatment. The texture is a surprise and the taste is a bonus.

4   cups grated sweet potato
½   cup sugar
½   teaspoon ground cinnamon
¼   teaspoon salt
1   cup milk
¼   cup butter, melted
3   eggs, beaten

❶ Heat oven to 325°F. Spray 3-quart casserole with nonstick cooking spray.

❷ In large bowl, gently stir together sweet potato, sugar, cinnamon, salt, milk, butter and eggs until well combined. Pour mixture into casserole. Bake 1 hour.

6 servings.

JO'S SWEET POTATO CASSEROLE

ROSMARIE STROTHER
NAPLES, FLORIDA

One of my best friends, who has passed away, always served this casserole at Christmas. It's a favorite in my household among family and friends.

4   large sweet potatoes, baked, pulp removed
    and skin discarded
½   cup butter, sliced ¼ inch thick
1   cup granulated sugar
2   eggs, lightly beaten
1   teaspoon vanilla
1   cup packed brown sugar
⅓   cup all-purpose flour
1   cup chopped pecans
6   tablespoons butter, melted

❶ Heat oven to 350°F. Spray 8-inch square pan with nonstick cooking spray.

❷ Spoon sweet potato pulp into large bowl; blend in butter slices until melted. Stir in granulated sugar, eggs and vanilla. Pour mixture into pan.

❸ In medium bowl, combine brown sugar, flour and pecans; mix well. Stir in melted butter. Sprinkle brown sugar mixture over potatoes. Bake 30 to 35 minutes.

8 servings.

PHYLLIS PUTNAM'S CALICO BEANS

TAMI ZYLKA
BLUE BELL, PENNSYLVANIA

Each summer picnic must have this version of baked beans!

½   lb. ground beef
½   cup chopped onion
½   cup packed brown sugar
1   teaspoon dry mustard
1   teaspoon salt
½   cup ketchup
2   teaspoons cider vinegar
1   (16-oz.) can pork-n-beans, drained, rinsed
1   (15-oz.) can kidney beans, drained, rinsed
1   (15-oz.) can butter beans, drained, rinsed
6   thick slices bacon, cooked, crumbled

❶ Heat oven to 350°F. Spray 3-quart casserole with nonstick cooking spray.

❷ In large skillet, cook beef and onion over medium-high heat 8 to 10 minutes or until beef is evenly browned; drain.

❸ In large bowl, combine beef mixture, brown sugar, mustard, salt, ketchup, vinegar, pork-n-beans, kidney beans and butter beans; mix well.

❹ Spread mixture into bottom of casserole; sprinkle with bacon. Bake uncovered 40 minutes.

8 servings.

SPANAKORIZO

SPANAKORIZO

DAPHNE NIEBOER
GRAND RAPIDS, MICHIGAN

I enjoyed this recipe for spinach with rice while growing up. It's a recipe handed down from my father's Greek side of the family.

1   cup plus 2 tablespoons butter
2   large onions, chopped
2   teaspoons dried parsley
1   teaspoon celery salt
⅛   teaspoon salt
⅛   teaspoon freshly ground pepper
⅛   teaspoon paprika
1   chicken bouillon cube
½   cup tomato sauce
1½ cups water
2   (10-oz.) pkg. frozen chopped spinach
1   cup rice

❶ In large skillet, heat butter over medium heat until melted. Add onions; sauté 6 to 8 minutes or until tender. Add parsley, celery salt, salt, pepper, paprika, bouillon cube and tomato sauce; sauté 3 to 4 minutes. Add water and spinach; bring to a boil. Add rice. Reduce heat to a simmer; cover. Cook 20 minutes or until rice is tender.

6 servings.

KASHA AND BOWS

EILEEN SWARTZ
AVENTURA, FLORIDA

This side dish originated in our family with my great-grandmother. We serve it in our home on almost every Jewish holiday.

1   cup water
1   cup reduced-sodium chicken broth
1   egg, beaten
1   cup kasha (roasted buckwheat)
½   cup butter
1   medium onion, finely chopped
2   cups egg noodle bows, cooked
⅛   teaspoon salt
⅛   teaspoon freshly ground pepper

❶ In large pot, heat water and broth to a boil over medium-high heat. In small bowl, combine egg and kasha; mix well. In large saucepan, melt butter over medium heat. Add onion; cook until onion is lightly brown. Add kasha mixture; cook until brown. Add boiling liquid, cover saucepan tightly; simmer 8 to 11 minutes or until kasha is tender and all liquid is absorbed. Stir in noodles, salt and pepper.

4 servings.

PINEAPPLE NOODLE RING

NANCY WALKER
WOOD RIVER, ILLINOIS

This is my grandmother's recipe. I hope you enjoy it as much as I do.

¼   cup packed dark brown sugar
1   (16-oz.) can crushed pineapple, drained
8   oz. medium egg noodles, cooked
½   cup butter, melted
4   eggs, lightly beaten

❶ Heat oven to 325°F. Spray 6-cup ring mold with nonstick cooking spray.

❷ In small bowl, combine 2 tablespoons of the brown sugar and ¼ of the pineapple; mix well. Spread mixture into bottom of mold. In large bowl, combine noodles, remaining 2 tablespoons brown sugar, remaining pineapple, butter and eggs; mix well. Spoon noodle mixture into mold. Bake 1 hour. Turn out onto serving platter; serve hot.

8 servings.

POTATO STUFFING

RENAY WULPERN
SANFORD, NORTH CAROLINA

We serve this stuffing every year at Thanksgiving.

¼   lb. Italian sausage, casing removed
2   tablespoons olive oil
5   russet potatoes, peeled, diced
⅛   teaspoon salt
⅛   teaspoon freshly ground pepper
⅛   teaspoon Italian seasoning
1   onion, chopped
½   cup chopped green bell pepper
¼   cup chopped celery
¼   cup freshly grated Parmesan cheese
1   egg, lightly beaten

❶ Heat oven to 350°F. Spray 13x9-inch pan with nonstick cooking spray.

❷ In large skillet, brown sausage over medium-high heat. Remove sausage from skillet; drain. Place sausage in large bowl. In clean skillet, heat oil over medium-high heat until hot. Add potatoes, salt, ground pepper and Italian seasoning; cook 6 to 8 minutes or until potatoes are tender and browned. Remove mixture from skillet to bowl with sausage. Stir in onion, bell pepper, celery, Parmesan and egg. Spread mixture into pan. Bake 45 minutes. Serve with turkey or chicken.

12 servings.

POTATO CASSEROLE

DAVID RITTER
DOUGLASSVILLE, PENNSYLVANIA

My wife likes to serve this dish to coworkers she invites home for lunch. It's delicious and full of flavor.

6   medium potatoes, peeled, cooked and diced
¾   cup butter, melted
¾   cup pimientos, drained, chopped
½   cup green bell pepper, chopped
1   (12-oz.) can evaporated milk
¼   teaspoon freshly ground pepper
¾   cup (3 oz.) shredded cheddar cheese
1   cup fresh bread crumbs

❶ Heat oven to 350°F. Spray 13x9-inch pan with nonstick cooking spray.

❷ In large bowl, combine potatoes, ½ cup of the butter, pimientos, bell pepper, evaporated milk, ground pepper and cheddar; mix thoroughly. In small bowl, combine bread crumbs and remaining ¼ cup butter. Transfer potato mixture to pan; sprinkle with bread crumbs. Bake uncovered 30 minutes.

6 servings.

CORN DRESSING

RITA VAIL
LAKEWOOD, COLORADO

I've had many requests for my mother's corn dressing recipe. I serve it as a side dish.

8   slices bread, torn into bite-size pieces
¼   cup butter
1   cup chopped celery
½   cup chopped onion
1   (15-oz.) can cream-style corn
1   cup water
1   teaspoon salt
½   teaspoon poultry seasoning
¼   teaspoon freshly ground pepper
3   eggs, beaten

❶ Heat oven to 375°F. Spray 13x9-inch pan with nonstick cooking spray. Spread bread pieces in bottom of pan.

❷ In large skillet, melt butter over medium heat. Add celery and onion; sauté 5 to 7 minutes or until tender. Add corn, water, salt, poultry seasoning and pepper. Bring to a boil. Pour mixture over bread in pan. Mix lightly; gently stir in eggs. Bake 15 to 20 minutes.

8 servings.

SQUASH APPLE BAKE

REBEKAH MILLER
RUSSELLVILLE, ALABAMA

This delicious side dish often sits alongside the turkey and stuffing on our Thanksgiving table.

2   lb. butternut squash, halved, seeded, peeled and sliced
2   baking apples, cored, peeled
½   cup packed brown sugar
1   tablespoon all-purpose flour
1   teaspoon salt
½   teaspoon ground mace
¼   cup butter

❶ Arrange squash and apples in 13x9-inch pan.

❷ In large bowl, sift together brown sugar, flour, salt and mace; sprinkle over squash and apples. Dot with butter. Cover with aluminum foil. Bake 50 to 60 minutes or until squash is tender.

Serves 6.

BAKED CORN CASSEROLE

AUDREY DERR
VALRICO, FLORIDA

This was one of my mother-in-law's recipes. We always requested it when we had dinner at her place.

½   cup butter
2   cups bread cubes
1   medium onion, chopped
1   green bell pepper, chopped
¼   cup all-purpose flour
1½ teaspoons salt
½   teaspoon dry mustard
¼   teaspoon freshly ground pepper
2   to 2¼ cups milk
4   cups frozen corn, thawed, or canned corn, drained
1   egg, lightly beaten

❶ Heat oven to 325°F. Spray 1½-quart casserole with nonstick cooking spray. In small skillet, heat ¼ cup of the butter over medium heat until melted. Add bread cubes; sauté until browned. Set aside.

❷ In large skillet, heat remaining ¼ cup butter until melted. Add onion and bell pepper; sauté until onion is transparent. Stir in flour, salt, mustard and ground pepper until blended. Add milk; cook until mixture has thickened. Add half of the bread cubes, corn and egg; mix thoroughly. Pour mixture into casserole. Sprinkle with remaining half bread cubes. Bake uncovered 45 minutes.

8 servings.

SQUASH APPLE BAKE

TEXICAN HOMINY

TEXICAN HOMINY
FAY COLEMAN
WACO, TEXAS

This is a great side dish, but I sometimes use Texican Hominy *as a main dish served with a green salad. It's very popular with picnic crowds.*

¼   cup olive oil
1   lb. thick-sliced bacon, cooked, crumbled,
       drippings reserved
1   medium onion, chopped
1   each yellow, red and green bell peppers, chopped
2   to 3 ribs celery, chopped
½   teaspoon ground cumin
2   garlic cloves, finely chopped
1   (10-oz.) can tomatoes with chiles
2   (15.5-oz.) cans golden hominy or
       1 (15.5-oz.) can white hominy, drained
1   (15.5-oz.) can black beans (optional), drained, rinsed

❶ In large skillet, heat oil and reserved bacon drippings (about 2 tablespoons) over medium-high heat until hot. Add onion, bell peppers, celery, cumin and garlic; sauté until onion is tender. Add tomatoes with chiles; simmer gently until most of the liquid has absorbed. Add hominy and beans, if using; simmer 5 minutes or until flavors blend. Stir in bacon.

16 servings.

SWEET AND SOUR GREEN BEANS WITH BACON
JULIE SCHMIDT
SUN PRAIRIE, WISCONSIN

My mother always made this when green beans were fresh from the garden. It's absolutely wonderful with beef, pork or chicken.

½   lb. thick-sliced bacon, cut into 1-inch pieces
1   lb. green beans
2   tablespoons cider vinegar
¼   cup sugar
⅛   teaspoon salt
⅛   teaspoon freshly ground pepper

❶ Heat large skillet over medium heat until hot. Add bacon; cook 6 to 8 minutes or until crisp. Remove from heat. Drain bacon; set aside. Steam beans until fork-tender.

❷ In large bowl, combine bacon, beans, vinegar and sugar; toss well. Season with salt and pepper.

6 servings.

CINNAMON CORN CASSEROLE
STEVEN ELLISON
JACKSONVILLE, ARKANSAS

My mother started this recipe and always served it on Thanksgiving. It is an Ellison tradition.

CASSEROLE
½   cup butter, melted
½   cup sugar
1   tablespoon all-purpose flour
1½ teaspoons baking powder
½   cup evaporated milk
2   (16-oz.) cans whole kernel corn, drained
2   eggs, beaten

TOPPING
¼   cup sugar
½   teaspoon ground cinnamon

❶ Heat oven to 350°F. Spray 3-quart casserole with nonstick cooking spray.

❷ For Casserole: In large bowl, combine butter, ½ cup sugar, flour, baking powder, evaporated milk, corn and eggs; mix well. Pour mixture into casserole. For Topping: In small bowl, combine ¼ cup sugar and cinnamon; sprinkle sugar mixture evenly over casserole. Bake, uncovered, 45 to 60 minutes or until topping is deep golden brown.

8 servings.

SPINACH CASSEROLE
CHRISTINE JONES
AKRON, OHIO

I love to make this recipe just as much as my family and friends love to eat it.

2   (10-oz.) pkg. frozen chopped spinach
1   (8-oz.) pkg. cream cheese, softened
½   cup butter, softened
½   teaspoon garlic powder
½   teaspoon seasoned salt
¼   teaspoon freshly ground pepper
¼   cup dry seasoned bread crumbs
2   tablespoons freshly grated Parmesan cheese
1   teaspoon butter, melted

❶ Heat oven to 350°F. Spray 8-inch square pan with nonstick cooking spray.

❷ In small pot, cook spinach according to package directions; drain and pat dry. In large bowl, combine spinach, cream cheese, softened butter, garlic powder, seasoned salt and pepper; mix well. Spread mixture into pan. In medium bowl, combine bread crumbs, Parmesan and melted butter; mix well. Sprinkle mixture over casserole. Bake uncovered 30 minutes.

6 servings.

TURKEY DRESSING CARLOTTA

CHARLOTTE WARD
HILTON HEAD ISLAND, SOUTH CAROLINA

In a creative mood one Thanksgiving, I wanted to have a traditional turkey dressing sparked with unique flavor. This was the result and now it's our favorite.

¼ cup olive oil
1 cup chopped onion
1 cup chopped celery
1 cup sliced mushrooms
6 thick slices bacon, cooked, crumbled
1 cup cranberries
1 cup dried apricots, chopped
1 cup finely chopped pecans
4 cups bread cubes (preferably homemade and a
  mixture of white, whole wheat and rye)
1 cup reduced-sodium chicken broth, plus more if needed
2 eggs, beaten
1½ teaspoons salt
½ teaspoon poultry seasoning
½ teaspoon sage
½ teaspoon thyme
½ teaspoon freshly ground pepper

❶ Heat oven to 350°F. Spray 2 (9-inch) square pans with nonstick cooking spray.

❷ In large skillet, heat oil over medium-high heat until hot. Add onion, celery and mushrooms; sauté 5 to 7 minutes or until tender. Remove from heat. Pour onion mixture into large bowl. Stir in bacon, cranberries, apricots, pecans, bread cubes, 1 cup broth, eggs, salt, poultry seasoning, sage, thyme and pepper; mix well. (If mixture seems too dry, add more broth as needed until mixture holds together well, but is not soggy.) Spread mixture into pans. Bake covered 20 minutes. Uncover; bake 10 minutes more.

10 to 12 servings (enough for 10- to 12-lb. turkey).

LIMA BEAN AND CELERY SAUTE

WILLY WILKINS
RICHMOND HILL, ONTARIO, CANADA

This recipe was created for a group that arrived for an afternoon cocktail but ended up staying for dinner. The recipe changes frequently according to what's available in the refrigerator or pantry!

4 cups fresh green beans, trimmed, cut into 1-inch pieces
5 thick slices bacon
4 ribs celery, sliced into ½-inch pieces
1 medium onion, chopped
2 garlic cloves, minced
1 to 2 tablespoons chopped fresh ginger (optional)
6 tablespoons chopped fresh parsley
1 tablespoon fresh oregano
⅛ teaspoon salt
⅛ teaspoon freshly ground pepper
2 tablespoons soy sauce
2 tablespoons butter (optional)
1 (19-oz.) can baby lima beans, drained, rinsed

❶ In small pot, cook green beans in small amount of water until just crisp-tender. Drain; set aside.

❷ Heat large skillet over medium heat until hot. Add bacon; cook 4 to 6 minutes or until crisp; set aside. Do not drain bacon drippings. To skillet, add celery, onion, garlic, ginger, if using, parsley, oregano, salt and pepper. Cook 7 minutes or until celery is crisp-tender. Add soy sauce. If pan is still somewhat dry, add butter, 1 teaspoon at a time. Reduce heat to low. Add green beans, bacon and lima beans. Cook 2 to 3 minutes or until lima beans are heated through. Serve immediately.

6 servings.

ONE-DISH SUPPERS

MACARONI AND CHEESE WITH TOMATO

ANITA COYNE
BONITA SPRINGS, FLORIDA

Growing up Catholic, we always had meatless Friday nights. My family's favorite dish was Mom's macaroni and cheese with a twist—tomatoes.

1   (16-oz.) pkg. macaroni
1   cup soft bread crumbs
1   cup diced American cheese
⅓   cup diced green bell pepper
1   teaspoon grated onion
¼   cup margarine, melted
2   eggs, beaten
1   (14½-oz.) can diced tomatoes
⅛   teaspoon salt
⅛   teaspoon freshly ground pepper

❶ Heat oven to 325°F. Spray 2-quart casserole with nonstick cooking spray.

❷ In large pot, cook macaroni according to package directions. Drain; rinse. Return to pot; add bread crumbs, cheese, bell pepper, onion, margarine, eggs and tomatoes; mix lightly. Season with salt and pepper. Pour mixture into casserole. Bake covered 45 minutes.

6 to 8 servings.

BAKED MACARONI AND CHEESE

JANE ZIMMERMAN
CHICAGO, ILLINOIS

This recipe always gets rave reviews in my family, and far surpasses anything else by the same name.

MACARONI
8   oz. miniature penne
8   oz. extra-sharp cheddar cheese, grated
1   tablespoon grated onion
½   teaspoon dry mustard
1   teaspoon Worcestershire sauce
    Dash paprika

WHITE SAUCE
3   tablespoons butter
2   tablespoons all-purpose flour
1   teaspoon salt
¼   teaspoon freshly ground pepper
2   cups milk

❶ Cook penne according to package directions. Drain; rinse. Heat oven to 375°F. Spray 3-quart casserole with nonstick spray.

❷ For Sauce: In large saucepan, melt butter over low heat. Add flour, salt and pepper. Stir until blended; remove from heat. Gradually whisk in milk; return to heat. Cook, stirring constantly, until thick and smooth.

❸ In large bowl, combine sauce, cheddar (reserve some for topping), onion, mustard and Worcestershire. Stir in penne. Pour mixture into casserole; top with reserved cheddar and paprika. Bake 25 minutes or until browned.

4 to 6 servings.

BAKED MACARONI

JOHN AND PAULA MOORE
LEECHBURG, PENNSYLVANIA

My grandmother served this recipe in her Leechburg restaurant.

¼   vegetable oil
1   small onion, finely chopped
1   medium red or green bell pepper, finely chopped
3½ cups water
1   (28-oz.) can crushed tomatoes in puree
1   (16-oz.) pkg. rotini, cooked, drained, rinsed
⅛   teaspoon salt
⅛   teaspoon freshly ground pepper
10 slices American cheese

❶ Heat oven to 350°F. In large saucepan, heat oil over medium-high heat until hot. Add onion and bell pepper; sauté 10 minutes or until tender. Stir in water and tomatoes. Cover bottom of 3-quart casserole with some of the sauce. Add half of the rotini. Sprinkle with salt and pepper. Cover with 5 slices of the cheese. Top with more sauce, remaining half of rotini, 5 slices cheese and sauce. Sprinkle with salt and pepper. Bake 1 hour or until sauce has thickened. Let stand 10 to 15 minutes before serving.

6 to 8 servings.

BAKED TUNA WITH CHEESE BISCUITS

PAULA KOHLHOFF
OSHKOSH, WISCONSIN

This was my mom's recipe. She passed away in 1986. I think of her every time I make it.

3   tablespoons butter
1   medium onion, chopped
1   medium green bell pepper, chopped
6   tablespoons all-purpose flour
3   cups milk
1   teaspoon salt
⅛   teaspoon freshly ground pepper
2   (7-oz.) cans tuna, drained
2   cups buttermilk baking mix
½   cup water
¾   cup grated cheddar cheese

❶ Heat oven to 375°F. In large skillet, melt butter over medium heat. Add onion and bell pepper; sauté until tender. Stir in flour until well blended. Gradually whisk in milk. Season with salt and pepper. Cook, stirring constantly, until sauce bubbles. Add tuna. Transfer mixture to 13x9-inch pan.

❷ In medium bowl, prepare baking mix with water until dough is formed; pat out on lightly floured board. Shape dough into ½-inch-thick rectangle. Sprinkle with cheddar. Roll up jelly-roll fashion; slice. Arrange slices on top of tuna mixture. Bake 30 minutes or until cheese biscuits are golden brown.

6 servings.

VEGETARIAN TOMATO, MUSHROOM AND RICE-STUFFED PEPPERS

RHEA NEWMAN
SHERMAN OAKS, CALIFORNIA

When I was 12 years old, my Russian grandmother made this for me. I'm now in my 70s, and am still making it.

4   green bell peppers
2   cups cooked rice
2   (4-oz.) cans sliced mushrooms, drained
1   (15-oz.) can stewed tomatoes
1   large can tomato sauce

❶ Heat oven to 350°F. In large pot, cook bell peppers in water over medium heat 5 minutes; drain peppers. Cut tops from peppers; place peppers in pan. Fill peppers with 1 layer each of rice, mushrooms and tomatoes; pour tomato sauce over each. Bake 45 minutes or until peppers are tender. Serve with salad and baked potato.

4 servings.

WILD RICE CASSEROLE

MARY HORSAGER
VERNDALE, MINNESOTA

This family favorite can be frozen ahead of time. It came from a friend many years ago.

1   cup uncooked wild rice
3   cups diced cooked turkey or chicken
2   cups sliced mushrooms with liquid
½   cup almonds, chopped
1   large onion, chopped
½   teaspoon salt
¼   teaspoon onion salt
¼   teaspoon garlic salt
¼   teaspoon celery salt
¼   teaspoon dried thyme
¼   teaspoon paprika
¼   teaspoon freshly ground pepper
1½   cups milk or water
2   (10¾-oz.) cans cream of chicken soup
1   teaspoon dried parsley

❶ Heat oven to 350°F.

❷ In large bowl, mix together rice, turkey, mushrooms, almonds, onion, salt, onion salt, garlic salt, celery salt, thyme, paprika, pepper, milk and soup. Spoon mixture into 13x9-inch pan; sprinkle with parsley. Cover with aluminum foil; bake 1 hour. Uncover; bake 2 hours. Refrigerate to cool; reheat before serving.

12 servings.

HOMEMADE MEDITERRANEAN PIZZA

IRAM AHMED
BOARDMAN, OHIO

I remember Mom making this pizza for me when I was a child.

CRUST
1 cup warm water (105ºF to 115ºF)
1 (¼-oz.) pkg. active dry yeast
2 to 2½ cups all-purpose flour
½ teaspoon salt
2 teaspoons olive oil
  White cornmeal

SAUCE
1 tablespoon olive oil
3 garlic cloves, chopped
2 cups chopped tomatoes
½ cup reduced-sodium chicken broth
2 tablespoons tomato paste
3 tablespoons fresh basil, chopped
1 teaspoon sugar
  Salt and freshly ground pepper to taste

TOPPINGS
2 cups (8 oz.) shredded mozzarella cheese
½ red bell pepper, sliced into rings
½ yellow bell pepper, sliced into rings
½ green bell pepper, sliced into rings
1 small onion, sliced
  Shredded Parmesan cheese
½ teaspoon dried oregano
3 sun-dried tomatoes, chopped
  Olive oil for drizzling

❶ For Crust: Pour hot water into large bowl. After a few minutes, discard water. Add 1 cup warm water and yeast to bowl. Add flour, ½ teaspoon salt and 2 teaspoons oil; mix until dough pulls away from sides of bowl. Put dough in large greased bowl; cover with plastic wrap. Let rise in warm place, away from drafts, 3 to 4 hours.

❷ For Sauce: In large skillet, heat 1 tablespoon oil over medium-high heat. Add garlic; sauté 1 minute. Add chopped tomatoes; sauté 2 minutes. Add broth; bring to a boil. Stir in tomato paste, basil, sugar, salt and pepper. Cover; simmer about 30 minutes. Heat oven to 450ºF.

❸ For Topping: Sprinkle pizza stone or deep-dish pizza pan with cornmeal. Spread risen dough onto stone, pinching edges to form crust; top with sauce. Sprinkle with 1½ cups of the mozzarella, bell peppers, onion, remaining ½ cup mozzarella, Parmesan, oregano and sun-dried tomatoes. Drizzle with oil. Bake 15 to 18 minutes or until cheese bubbles.

6 servings.

PASTA PUTTANESCA

HARMONY TARDUGNO
ROME, NEW YORK

My husband first prepared this for me when we were dating. It is my favorite pasta sauce.

2 tablespoons extra-virgin olive oil
2 anchovy fillets
2 garlic cloves, minced
1 (14½-oz.) can imported whole plum tomatoes
½ cup Kalamata olives, halved
2 tablespoons capers, drained
1 tablespoon dried basil
⅛ teaspoon salt
⅛ teaspoon freshly ground pepper
8 oz. pasta, cooked, drained
  Pecorino cheese, freshly grated

❶ In large skillet, heat oil over medium heat until hot. Add anchovies and garlic; cook 2 to 3 minutes until anchovies are melted. Add tomatoes, breaking them up with spoon. Cook 10 to 15 minutes. Reduce heat; add olives, capers, basil, salt and pepper. Cook 10 to 15 minutes to infuse flavors. Toss with pasta; garnish with pecorino to serve.

4 servings.

PASTA PUTTANESCA

STUFFED MANICOTTI

SUSAN BORK
INDIANAPOLIS, INDIANA

My sister-in-law shared this recipe with me and today I use it for company as well as my family.

SAUCE

1½ lb. ground round
1   cup chopped onion
2   garlic cloves, minced
¼   cup fresh parsley, chopped
2   tablespoons dried basil
1½ teaspoons salt
⅛   teaspoon freshly ground pepper
4   cups water
4   (6-oz.) cans tomato paste

FILLING

1½ lb. cottage cheese, drained
⅔   cup freshly grated Parmesan cheese
2   eggs, lightly beaten
¼   cup dried parsley
½   teaspoon salt
⅛   teaspoon freshly ground pepper

PASTA

1   (8-oz.) pkg. manicotti shells
½   cup freshly grated Parmesan cheese

❶ For Sauce: In large skillet, brown meat lightly over medium-high heat; drain. Add onion, garlic, fresh parsley, basil, 1½ teaspoons salt, pepper, water and tomato paste. Simmer uncovered 30 minutes.

❷ Meanwhile, prepare Filling: Heat oven to 350°F. In large bowl, combine cottage cheese, ⅔ cup Parmesan, eggs, dried parsley, ½ teaspoon salt and pepper. Stuff shells with filling. Spread half of meat mixture into bottom of 13x9-inch pan. Arrange stuffed shells in a row over meat mixture; top with remaining half meat mixture. Sprinkle with ½ cup Parmesan. Bake 35 to 45 minutes.

4 to 6 servings.

PASTELON

PETER BERNASCONI
BRONX, NEW YORK

This recipe is special to my wife and me because my father-in-law made it for us when we were in Puerto Rico. We enjoy plantains fried, baked or boiled. It's easy to make and delicious!

½   cup vegetable oil
8   to 10 yellow sweet plantains, jeweled, sliced horizontally
1½ lb. ground meat
⅛   teaspoon salt
⅛   teaspoon freshly ground pepper
¼   to ½ cup pimiento-stuffed green olives
1   (14½-oz.) can tomato sauce
1   (16-oz.) pkg. shredded mozzarella cheese

❶ In large skillet, heat oil over medium-high heat until hot. Add plantains; fry until golden brown. Drain on paper towels. Season meat with salt and pepper. In clean skillet, brown meat; add olives and tomato sauce. Simmer about 15 minutes.

❷ Heat oven to 350°F. In 15x10x1-inch baking pan, layer plantains, meat mixture and mozzarella as if making lasagna. Bake 30 minutes. Serve hot with salad on the side.

6 servings.

TOMATO LASAGNA ROLL-UPS

ANN MCCARTHY
BELFAST, NEW YORK

*These roll-ups are easy to make, and they freeze beautifully
in individual packages for a quick lunch or supper.*

8   lasagna noodles
2   tablespoons olive oil
¼   cup finely chopped onion
1¾ cups stewed tomatoes
⅔   cup tomato paste
1¾ cups ricotta cheese
1¼ cups frozen chopped spinach, thawed, drained
1   cup (4 oz.) shredded mozzarella cheese
1   egg, lightly beaten
2   tablespoons freshly grated Parmesan cheese
½   teaspoon salt
¼   teaspoon freshly ground pepper

❶ Cook noodles according to package directions.
Rinse; drain. Lay noodles flat on aluminum foil to
cool. Heat oven to 350°F.

❷ In large skillet, heat oil over medium-high until
hot. Add onion; cook, stirring frequently, until
tender. Add tomatoes and tomato paste; heat to a
boil. Reduce heat; simmer 5 minutes, stirring to
break up tomatoes. Set aside.

❸ In large bowl, stir together ricotta, spinach, ½ cup
of the mozzarella, egg, Parmesan, salt and pepper.
Spread ¾ cup of the tomato sauce into bottom of
13x9-inch pan. Spread ⅓ cup cheese mixture on
each noodle to within 1 inch of ends; roll up. Place
roll-ups seam-side down in pan; top with
remaining tomato sauce. Bake covered 35 minutes
or until hot and bubbly. Sprinkle with the
remaining ½ cup mozzarella; continue baking
until cheese melts.

6 servings.

TRUE ITALIAN LASAGNA

MARY BLESSING
NORTH VERNON, INDIANA

*My sister and I combined recipes and came up with this
family favorite.*

1   lb. sweet Italian sausage
1   garlic clove, chopped
1   teaspoon dried basil
1   (14-oz.) can whole tomatoes, coarsely chopped
2   (6-oz.) cans tomato paste
1   (10-oz.) pkg. lasagna noodles
3   cups ricotta cheese
½   cup freshly grated Parmesan
2   teaspoons dried parsley
2   eggs, beaten
½   teaspoon salt
½   teaspoon freshly ground pepper
1   lb. mozzarella cheese, sliced

❶ In large skillet, brown sausage slowly over
medium-high heat; spoon off fat. Add garlic, basil,
tomatoes and tomato paste; stir to blend. Simmer
uncovered 30 minutes, stirring frequently.

❷ Cook noodles according to package directions.
Rinse; drain. Heat oven to 350°F.

❸ In large bowl, mix together ricotta, Parmesan,
parsley, eggs, salt and pepper; set aside. In 13x9-
inch pan, arrange 1 layer each of noodles, ricotta
mixture, sauce and mozzarella. Repeat layers until
ingredients are gone, ending with mozzarella on
top. Bake 40 to 45 minutes. Remove from oven; let
stand 10 minutes.

4 to 6 servings.

ITALIAN WEDDING SOUP

ITALIAN WEDDING SOUP

HARMONY TARDUGNO
ROME, NEW YORK

Here's a re-created favorite that my family never grows bored of.

SOUP
1 (4-lb.) stewing chicken
4 quarts cold water
1 tablespoon salt
4 outer ribs celery
2 large onions, chopped
12 peppercorns
2 garlic cloves, minced
2 bay leaves
  Fresh parsley
1 to 2 bunches escarole, washed

MEATBALLS
1 lb. ground beef
½ cup bread crumbs
2 tablespoons freshly grated Parmesan cheese, plus
    more for topping
1 tablespoon dried parsley
½ teaspoon dried basil
⅛ teaspoon salt
⅛ teaspoon freshly ground pepper
1 egg, beaten

❶ For Soup: Wash chicken pieces; place in 8-quart pot. Cover with cold water; add salt. Cover pot; bring to a boil over medium-high heat. Skim foam, simmering until foam no longer appears. Reduce heat; add 2 of the ribs celery, 1 of the onions, peppercorns, garlic, bay leaves and fresh parsley. Simmer slowly 2 hours or until chicken is cooked.

❷ Meanwhile, prepare Meatballs: In large bowl, mix together beef, bread crumbs, Parmesan, dried parsley, basil, salt, pepper and egg. Shape into miniature meatballs.

❸ In large pot of water, boil escarole until tender; drain. Squeeze all water out; cut into small pieces. Chop remaining 2 ribs celery and onion; set aside. When chicken is cooked, strain stock; discard vegetables, peppercorns and bay leaves. Remove chicken from bones; cut meat into small pieces. Set aside. Return stock to pot; add chopped celery, onion, and escarole. Boil until vegetables are tender. Drop in meatballs; cook 7 minutes or until they are done and float to top. Serve soup in bowls topped with Parmesan.

12 servings.

GRANDMA DODGE'S LASAGNA

LETHA MELLMAN
ROY, UTAH

This recipe is from my grandma, Sara Dodge. It is one of the first things my mom learned to cook and one of the first things she passed on to me.

MEAT SAUCE
½ cup olive oil
1 medium onion
1 garlic clove
1½ lb. ground beef
1 (16-oz.) can tomatoes
2 (6-oz.) cans tomato paste
1 teaspoon dried oregano
⅛ teaspoon salt
⅛ teaspoon freshly ground pepper
1 bay leaf

WHITE SAUCE
¼ cup butter
¼ cup all-purpose flour
2 cups milk

LASAGNA
1 (16-oz.) pkg. lasagna noodles, cooked, drained
1 cup shredded Parmesan cheese
1 (8-oz.) pkg. shredded mozzarella cheese
1 lb. ricotta cheese

❶ For Meat Sauce: In large skillet, heat oil over medium-high heat until hot. Add onion, garlic and beef; cook until beef is brown. Add tomatoes, tomato paste, oregano, salt, pepper and bay leaf. Cover; simmer 30 to 60 minutes or until sauce is no longer runny. Remove bay leaf.

❷ For White Sauce: In medium saucepan, melt butter over medium-high heat. Stir in flour. Add milk, whisking constantly, until thick and bubbly.

❸ Heat oven to 350°F. In 13x9-inch pan, layer ⅓ meat sauce, ⅓ noodles, ⅓ meat sauce, ½ cup of the Parmesan, ⅓ noodles, half of the mozzarella, white sauce, ⅓ noodles, ricotta, ⅓ meat sauce, remaining half of mozzarella and ½ cup Parmesan. Bake 30 to 45 minutes or until bubbly and cheese is melted.

6 to 8 servings.

BASIL LASAGNA

TERESA BELL
PITTSBURGH, PENNSYLVANIA

This recipe is the result of wanting to use fresh basil in a garlic cream sauce. It has turned out to be a family favorite.

8   lasagna noodles
¼   cup butter
2   garlic cloves, crushed
3   tablespoons all-purpose flour
    Dash ground nutmeg
2   cups milk
¼   cup fresh basil, finely chopped
2   cups ricotta cheese
1   cup freshly grated Parmesan cheese
⅛   teaspoon salt
⅛   teaspoon freshly ground pepper
1   (8-oz.) pkg. mozzarella cheese, sliced

❶ Cook noodles according to package directions. Rinse; drain. Heat oven to 375°F.

❷ In large saucepan, melt butter over medium-high heat. Add garlic; sauté until tender. Stir in flour and nutmeg. Add milk. Cook, stirring frequently, until thickened and bubbly. Cook, stirring, an additional 1 minute; remove from heat. Stir in 2 tablespoons of the basil. Add ricotta and ½ cup of the Parmesan, stirring until well combined. Season with salt and white pepper. Layer 4 of the noodles in 3-quart casserole. Spread with half of the cheese mixture; top with half of the mozzarella. Sprinkle with 1 tablespoon of the basil. Repeat layers, sprinkling remaining ½ cup Parmesan on top. Bake 30 to 35 minutes or until heated through. Let stand 10 minutes.

6 servings.

CHILI

TOMMIE COULTER
FORNEY, TEXAS

This is my husband's favorite. I make a double batch and freeze servings in freezer bags.

2   to 3 lb. chili meat
1   large onion, chopped
2   garlic cloves, minced
3   tablespoons chili powder
1   tablespoon ground cumin
1   teaspoon dried oregano
4   cups boiling water
4   cups tomato juice
1   (28-oz.) can crushed tomatoes
1   (14½-oz.) can tomato sauce
2   bay leaves
1   tablespoon salt
1   teaspoon freshly ground pepper
¼   cup water
3   tablespoons all-purpose flour

❶ In large skillet, brown meat over medium-high heat. Add onion and garlic; cook until onion is transparent. Stir in chili powder, cumin and oregano; mix well. Add boiling water, tomato juice, tomatoes, tomato sauce, bay leaves, salt and pepper. Bring to a boil, mixing well. Reduce heat; simmer 45 minutes. In measuring glass, whisk together ¼ cup water and flour; stir into chili. Heat until thickened. Remove bay leaves.

8 to 10 servings.

MOM'S CHICKEN SOUP

LINDA MANIA
OCALA, FLORIDA

This recipe never ceases to please!

1   (3½- to 4-lb.) stewing chicken
    About 10 cups water
1   lb. carrots, chopped
3   leeks, chopped
1   large onion, chopped
1   rib celery, chopped
1   tablespoon dried parsley
⅛   teaspoon salt
⅛   teaspoon freshly ground pepper

❶ In large pot, combine chicken and water. Cover; bring to a boil. Stir in carrots, leeks, onion, celery, parsley, salt and pepper. Cook until chicken is tender, about 2 hours; remove chicken to cool. Remove meat from bones. Dice chicken; return to soup.

6 to 8 servings.

TURKEY VEGETABLE SOUP CARLOTTA

CHARLOTTE WARD
HILTON HEAD ISLAND, SOUTH CAROLINA

This soup is a great comfort!

1	large turkey carcass, skinned
2	large turkey wings and legs, skinned
5	(16-oz.) cans reduced-sodium chicken broth
1	cup chopped celery
1	cup chopped onion
2	bay leaves
2	teaspoons salt
¼	teaspoon garlic powder
¼	teaspoon freshly ground pepper
2	tablespoons packed brown sugar
2	tablespoons Worcestershire sauce
1	tablespoon lemon juice
1	beef bouillon cube
1	cup peas, canned or frozen
1	cup cut green beans, canned or frozen
1	cup sliced mushrooms
1	cup pearl barley
1	(16-oz.) can small white potatoes, drained
1	(16-oz.) can sliced carrots, drained
1	(16-oz.) can crushed tomatoes
1	(16-oz.) can cream-style corn

❶ In large pot, combine turkey carcass, wings and legs, broth, celery, onion, bay leaves, salt, garlic powder, pepper, brown sugar, Worcestershire, lemon juice and bouillon cube. Bring to a boil over medium-high heat; simmer 2 hours. Remove turkey; shred meat. Return meat to soup; add peas, beans, mushrooms, barley, potatoes, carrots, tomatoes and corn. Bring to a boil; simmer 30 minutes. Remove bay leaves.

8 to 10 servings.

TORTILLA SOUP

DEANNA WHEELER
LONGMONT, COLORADO

Here's a soup that's sure to please your family and guests.

¼	cup vegetable oil
12	(6-inch) tortillas, cut into strips
1	(3¼- to 4-lb.) chicken
8	cups water
1	onion, quartered
1	teaspoon celery salt
1	teaspoon peppercorns
2	garlic cloves, peeled
2	serrano chiles, seeded, finely chopped
1	green bell pepper, chopped
½	bunch fresh cilantro
½	teaspoon ground cumin
8	green onions, chopped
2	cups cooked rice
⅛	teaspoon salt
1	lb. cheddar cheese, shredded
1	ripe avocado, chopped
	Cayenne pepper (optional)

❶ In large skillet, heat oil over medium-high heat until hot. Add tortilla strips; brown. Drain on paper towels.

❷ In large pot, combine chicken, water, onion, celery salt, peppercorns and garlic. Cover; bring to a boil. Reduce heat; simmer about 2 hours. Remove chicken from broth to cool. Strain stock; return to pot. Add serrano chiles, bell pepper, cilantro and cumin. Cover; simmer 30 minutes. Add green onions; simmer 10 minutes.

❸ Meanwhile, remove skin and bone from cooled chicken; cut meat into bite-size pieces. Add chicken, rice and salt to soup; heat through. Sprinkle each bowl with cheese. Top cheese with soup, tortilla strips and avocado. Sprinkle with cayenne, if desired.

4 to 6 servings.

GRANDMA'S PASTINA SOUP

MICHELE WEIGEL
SOUTH LAKE TAHOE, CALIFORNIA

*My Italian grandmother used to make this for me when I
was young. As I grew older, I modified the recipe by adding
more of what I liked.*

8   to 10 cups hot water
3   tablespoons chicken bouillon granules
2   to 3 carrots, sliced
2   to 3 ribs celery, sliced
2   to 3 potatoes, peeled, cubed
1   onion, chopped
2   garlic cloves, minced
2   skinless boneless chicken breasts, cut into bite-size pieces
⅛   teaspoon salt
⅛   teaspoon freshly ground pepper
12   cups water
8   oz. acini di pepe (star pasta)
     Freshly grated Parmesan cheese

❶ In large pot, bring hot water and 2 tablespoons of
the bouillon to a boil. Add carrots, celery, potatoes,
onion, garlic, chicken, salt and pepper; boil 5 to 7
minutes. Reduce heat; simmer 35 to 40 minutes.

❷ About 10 minutes before soup is done, in another
large pot, bring 12 cups water and remaining
tablespoon bouillon to a boil. Add pasta; boil 9 to
12 minutes. Drain pasta; add to soup. Place in
large serving bowl. Add Parmesan; stir to blend
flavors.

6 to 8 servings.

MINESTRONE SOUP

VIOLET HARTLEY
MODESTO, CALIFORNIA

*My mother made this for me when I was young and I made
it for my children. Now, I make it for my grandchildren.*

1   tablespoon olive oil
3   links mild Italian sausage, sliced crosswise
1   cup chopped sweet onion
2   garlic cloves, minced
1   cup chopped carrots
1   teaspoon fresh basil
1   zucchini, sliced
1   yellow summer squash, sliced
2   (10-oz.) cans reduced-sodium beef broth
1   to 2 (8-oz.) cans diced Italian tomatoes
⅛   teaspoon salt
⅛   teaspoon ground white pepper
2   cups finely chopped cabbage
1   (15-oz.) can cannellini beans, undrained
½   cup Burgundy wine
1½   cups cooked rigatoni
     Freshly grated Parmesan cheese
     Chopped fresh parsley

❶ In large skillet, heat oil over medium-high until
hot. Add sausage; brown. Add onion, garlic,
carrots and basil; cook 5 minutes. Add zucchini,
summer squash, broth, tomatoes, salt and white
pepper. Bring to a boil; reduce heat. Cover; simmer
1 hour. Add cabbage, beans and wine; cook 20
minutes. Refrigerate to cool. Reheat before serving,
stirring in rigatoni, salt and white pepper. Top
with Parmesan and parsley.

4 servings.

PIZZA SOUP

LYNDA BURTON
HOUSTON, TEXAS

My family loves this hearty soup! The more it cooks, the more intense the flavors.

2   tablespoons unsalted butter
2   ribs celery, diced
1   medium onion, diced
½   medium green bell pepper, diced
2   tablespoons fresh Italian parsley, coarsely chopped
1   lb. extra-lean ground beef
1   (8-oz.) pkg. sage sausage,
      cut into ½-inch chunks
1   (8-oz.) pkg. mild or sweet Italian sausage,
      casing removed, chopped
5   (14½-oz.) cans diced tomatoes, undrained
1   (14½-oz.) can tomato sauce
1   (6-oz.) can tomato paste
1   (2½-oz.) can sliced ripe olives, drained
1   teaspoon fennel seeds
½   teaspoon anise seeds
⅛   teaspoon each kosher (coarse) salt, freshly
      ground pepper
⅛   Shredded mozzarella cheese

❶ In large pot, melt butter over low heat. Add celery, onion, bell pepper and parsley; sauté until vegetables are tender. Remove from pan; keep warm.

❷ In same pot, brown ground beef and sausages; drain well. Return vegetables to pot. Stir in tomatoes, tomato sauce, tomato paste and olives. Simmer 10 to 15 minutes, stirring frequently. Stir in fennel seeds, anise seeds, salt and pepper until well blended. Cover; simmer over low heat 15 to 20 minutes. Top with mozzarella. Serve with garlic bread.

6 to 8 servings.

PASTA E FAGIOLI

MARTINA PALLADINO
FLANDERS, NEW JERSEY

Here's our favorite low-fat soup recipe.

2   tablespoons olive oil
1   cup chopped onion
2   tablespoons crushed garlic
½   cup diced pancetta
3   cups chopped plum tomatoes
½   teaspoon salt
½   teaspoon dried oregano
½   teaspoon crushed red pepper
½   teaspoon freshly ground pepper
2   (15½-oz.) cans great northern beans, drained, rinsed
1   (48-oz.) can reduced-sodium chicken broth
2   cups small tube pasta
½   cup light cream
½   (6-oz.) can tomato paste
½   cup chopped fresh Italian parsley
      Freshly grated Parmesan cheese

❶ In large skillet, heat oil over high heat until hot. Add onion, garlic and pancetta; sauté 5 minutes or until onion is transparent, stirring constantly. Reduce heat. Add tomatoes; simmer 10 minutes or until tomatoes are tender. Add salt, oregano, crushed red pepper and ground pepper; simmer 5 minutes to blend flavors. Add beans and broth; bring to a boil. Reduce heat; cover. Simmer 10 minutes.

❷ Meanwhile, in large saucepan, cook pasta according to package directions. (Do not overcook; pasta should be slightly firm.) Drain; rinse. Return pasta to saucepan; spray with cooking spray. Set aside.

❸ In measuring glass, whisk together cream and tomato paste; add to soup while stirring with other hand. Simmer 5 minutes. Stir in parsley; top with Parmesan.

4 to 6 servings.

CHICKEN AND DUMPLINGS

CHICKEN AND DUMPLINGS

SHARON TOWERS
MANHATTAN, KANSAS

I have many warm memories of this recipe shared by my mom and paternal grandmother.

1 (3½- to 4-lb.) chicken
5 carrots, sliced
3 ribs celery, chopped
⅛ teaspoon salt
⅛ teaspoon freshly ground pepper
2 cups all-purpose flour
   Milk

❶ In Dutch oven, cover chicken with water; boil over medium heat until chicken falls off the bone. Remove chicken; let stock cool. Remove chicken from bone; return meat to Dutch oven. Add carrots, celery, salt and pepper. Simmer over low heat.

❷ In medium bowl, mix flour with just enough milk to make pastry dough. On floured surface, roll dough ¼ inch thick, using additional flour as needed. Cut pastry into squares; slowly add to simmering pot. Cook 45 to 60 minutes.

4 to 6 servings.

PASTA FASAUSAGE SOUP

BARBARA BARTOLOMEO
RADNOR, PENNSYLVANIA

Here's my version of pasta fagioli — Pasta Fasausage. *We like it made with hot Italian sausage, which makes it very spicy.*

¼ cup olive oil
2 medium onions, chopped
4 large garlic cloves
1 lb. hot Italian sausage, casing removed
1 (28-oz.) can peeled or crushed Italian tomatoes
2 tablespoons fresh parsley, chopped
2 tablespoons fresh basil, chopped
1½ quarts water, plus more if needed
3½ cups reduced-sodium chicken broth
1 (16-oz.) can garbanzo beans, drained, rinsed
2 ribs celery, sliced crosswise into ¼-inch pieces
⅛ teaspoon salt
⅛ teaspoon freshly ground pepper
1 (16-oz.) pkg. small elbow pasta

❶ In large skillet, heat oil over medium-high heat until hot. Add onions and garlic; sauté until garlic is golden. Remove from skillet. Roll sausage into small balls. Add to skillet; fry until brown.

❷ In food processor or blender, puree onion mixture, tomatoes, parsley and basil.

❸ In large pot, combine pureed mixture, sausage, water, broth, garbanzo beans, celery, salt and pepper; simmer about 1 hour. Add pasta; continue cooking, stirring often, 30 minutes, adding water if needed. Serve with crusty bread.

4 servings.

TORTELLINI SOUP

KAREN LEE
SACRAMENTO, CALIFORNIA

For a full meal, serve this soup with salad and bread. It's also great for camping if you keep it hot on the fire.

3 tablespoons olive oil
1½ lb. kielbasa
1 medium onion, diced
3 garlic cloves, chopped
1 lb. sliced mushrooms
2 green bell peppers, diced
2 red bell peppers, diced
1 cup freshly grated Parmesan cheese
¼ cup fresh Italian parsley, chopped
1 tablespoon fresh sage, chopped
1 tablespoon fresh basil, chopped
1 tablespoon fresh rosemary, chopped
½ lb. prosciutto, cut into matchstick-size strips
     (¼x¼x2 inches)
4 boneless skinless chicken breast halves, diced
1½ gallons reduced-sodium chicken broth
1 bay leaf
2 lb. fresh or frozen cheese-filled tortellini

❶ In large pot, heat oil over medium-high heat until hot. Add kielbasa, onion, garlic, mushrooms and green and red bell peppers; sauté until onion is transparent. Add Parmesan, parsley, sage, basil, rosemary, prosciutto, chicken, broth and bay leaf. Simmer 30 minutes. Return to a boil; add tortellini. Cook until tortellini is tender. Remove bay leaf.

8 servings.

CHICKEN VICTORIA SOUP

CHRISTY KINNEY
NEWTON, NEW JERSEY

Our close family friend, Ellen, developed this recipe. It's so delicious, I've been known to drive to the store in a blizzard to pick up ingredients for it!

3 tablespoons butter
1 rib celery, chopped
1 carrot, chopped
1 medium onion, chopped
1½ cups fresh mushrooms, sliced
1½ cups chopped cooked chicken
½ cup chopped pimientos
2 cups reduced-sodium chicken broth
3 tablespoons all-purpose flour
¼ cup water
1 tablespoon fresh tarragon, chopped
1 teaspoon dried basil
1 teaspoon onion salt
1 teaspoon celery salt
½ teaspoon dried thyme
1½ cups half-and-half

❶ In large saucepan, melt butter over medium-high heat. Add celery, carrot, onion and mushrooms; sauté 10 minutes. Add chicken, pimientos and broth; simmer 15 minutes. In small bowl, whisk together flour and water; stir into soup. Simmer until thickened. Add tarragon, basil, onion salt, celery salt and thyme; simmer 15 minutes. Stir in half-and-half; simmer an additional 15 minutes.

6 servings.

CREAM OF CAULIFLOWER SOUP

P.D. HODGE
MADISONVILLE, TENNESSEE

I've served this for years in antique coffee cups as the first course of the meal. It gets rave reviews, and new friends always beg for the recipe.

1 large head cauliflower, chopped into small pieces
¼ cup butter
1 lb. potatoes, peeled, diced
1 to 1½ quarts reduced-sodium chicken broth, warmed
1 cup heavy cream
⅛ teaspoon salt
⅛ teaspoon ground white pepper
1 tablespoon fresh parsley, chopped

❶ Cook cauliflower briefly in boiling water to blanch. In large pot, melt butter over medium-high heat. Stir in cauliflower; cook 2 to 3 minutes. Add potatoes and warm broth; bring to a boil. Reduce heat; simmer 1 hour. Remove from heat. Puree soup in blender or with immersion blender. Stir in cream; season with salt and white pepper. Garnish with parsley.

8 to 10 servings.

ITALIAN VEGETABLE SOUP

TONI FAUCHEUX
MANDEVILLE, LOUISIANA

Here's a twist on vegetable soup.

1   medium eggplant
⅛   teaspoon salt plus more to taste
3   tablespoons olive oil
1   medium onion, chopped
1   medium green bell pepper, chopped
1   medium red bell pepper, chopped
1   tablespoon chopped garlic
1   large zucchini, halved, sliced
1   large yellow summer squash, halved, sliced
½   teaspoon dried oregano
3   small bay leaves
6   to 7 cups reduced-sodium chicken broth
2   (14½-oz.) cans diced tomatoes with basil and
    oregano, undrained
2   tablespoons lemon juice
⅛   teaspoon freshly ground pepper
    Freshly grated Parmesan cheese (optional)

❶ Peel eggplant; cut into ½-inch cubes. Place cubes
in colander. Sprinkle with ⅛ teaspoon salt; let
drain 30 minutes. Rinse briefly.

❷ Meanwhile, in large skillet, heat oil over medium-
high heat until hot. Add onion and green and red bell
peppers; sauté until tender. Add garlic, zucchini,
summer squash, oregano, bay leaves, broth and
tomatoes. Cook 45 minutes or until vegetables are
tender. Season with lemon juice, additional salt and
pepper. Remove bay leaves. Garnish each bowl of
soup with Parmesan, if desired.

6 servings.

LENTIL SOUP

BARBARA BRANDEL
OCALA, FLORIDA

*This recipe has been in our family for years. We love it
during the winter months when the chill is in the air.*

3   to 4 thick slices bacon
1   large onion, chopped
2   to 3 carrots, diced
2   to 3 parsnips, diced
1   cup dried lentils, rinsed
1   (48-oz.) can reduced-sodium chicken broth
1   large potato, diced
    Salt and freshly ground pepper to taste
    Dash red wine vinegar (optional)

❶ In large skillet, sauté bacon and onion over
medium-high heat 3 minutes or until bacon crisps
and onion is transparent. Add carrots and
parsnips; sauté 3 to 5 minutes. Add lentils and
broth; bring mixture to a boil. Reduce heat; cover.
Simmer 1½ hours or until vegetables are tender.
Add potato; cook until tender. Season with salt
and pepper. Add vinegar, if using.

6 to 8 servings.

POTATO SOUP

NICOLE BAROWY
VIRGINIA BEACH, VIRGINIA

*This recipe came from my great-grandmother. It's excellent in
winter.*

2   tablespoons butter
½   cup chopped onion
3   large baking potatoes, diced
1   tablespoon salt
2   cups water
¼   cup all-purpose flour
1½ teaspoons paprika
1   cup sour cream
2½ cups milk
⅛   teaspoon salt
⅛   teaspoon freshly ground pepper
    Shredded cheese, for sprinkling

❶ In large saucepan, melt butter over medium heat.
Add onion; cook until tender. Add potatoes, salt
and water. Cover; cook 20 minutes or until
potatoes are tender.

❷ In small bowl, blend flour, paprika and sour cream
until smooth; stir into saucepan. Add milk; heat to
a boil, stirring. Cook 2 minutes; season with salt
and pepper. Sprinkle with cheese.

4 servings.

GREEK SOUP

NICOLE BAROWY
VIRGINIA BEACH, VIRGINIA

This recipe has been a family favorite for nine generations and counting!

8   cups reduced-sodium chicken broth
1¼   cups long-grain white rice
3   eggs, separated
     Juice of 3 lemons
⅛   teaspoon salt
⅛   teaspoon freshly ground pepper

❶ In large saucepan, bring broth to a boil over medium heat. Add rice; simmer about 20 minutes. Remove from heat. In small bowl, beat egg whites until peaks form. Slowly add yolks; continue beating. Slowly add lemon juice. Slowly beat in 2 cups of hot broth; gradually pour mixture into remaining broth in saucepan, whisking constantly, until well mixed. Season with salt and pepper.

4 servings.

CORN CHOWDER

JANET HUCK
HOYLETON, ILLINOIS

This recipe is a crowd pleaser!

3   to 4 slices bacon, cut into ¼-inch pieces
3   tablespoons butter
¼   cup diced onion
¼   cup all-purpose flour
½   teaspoon dill weed
¼   teaspoon freshly ground pepper
2   cups reduced-fat (2%) milk
1   cup reduced-sodium chicken broth
1   cup water
1   (15-oz.) can whole kernel corn
1   (15-oz.) can cream-style corn
     Chopped fresh parsley (optional)

❶ In large skillet, sauté bacon over medium-high heat until crisp; drain on paper towels. Set aside. In clean large skillet, melt butter over medium heat; sauté onion until tender but not brown. Sprinkle with flour, dill and pepper; cook, stirring, 1 minute. Add milk, broth and water. Cook, stirring, until thick and bubbly. Cook an additional 1 minute. Add bacon and corn; heat through. Garnish with parsley, if desired. Serve with crusty French or dill bread.

4 servings.

CREAM OF WILD RICE SOUP

CHARLOTTE WARD
HILTON HEAD ISLAND, SOUTH CAROLINA

This soup comes close to the superb original I tasted in Minnesota years ago.

1½   cups butter
2   large onions, chopped
6   ribs celery, with leaves, chopped
1   lb. sliced fresh mushrooms
½   cup all-purpose flour
2   teaspoons salt
1   teaspoon cracked black pepper
½   gallon whole milk
3½   cups cooked wild rice

❶ In large skillet, melt 1 cup of the butter over medium heat. Add onions; sauté 5 minutes. Add celery and mushrooms; sauté until vegetables are tender. Set aside.

❷ In large Dutch oven, melt remaining ½ cup butter over medium-high heat. Gradually add flour, salt and pepper, stirring until smooth. Cook 1 minute, stirring constantly. Reduce heat to medium; gradually add milk. Cook, stirring constantly, until mixture is thickened and bubbly. Stir in sautéed vegetables and wild rice. Reduce heat to low; simmer 15 minutes.

6 servings.

CREAM OF WHOLE TOMATO SOUP

KATHERINE LANGWORTHY
THREE RIVERS, MICHIGAN

This is a family recipe we often prepare on Christmas Eve.

1   quart home-canned tomatoes
1   tablespoon dried onions (optional)
½   teaspoon baking soda
1   (12-oz.) can evaporated milk
⅛   teaspoon salt
⅛   teaspoon freshly ground pepper

❶ In medium pot, heat tomatoes and dried onions over medium-high heat. Stir in baking soda. Add evaporated milk; season with salt and pepper. Heat, but do not boil.

4 servings.

BREADS

WHOLE WHEAT BUNS

ROSE BOWERS
LOVETTSVILLE, VIRGINIA

This recipe was given to me in the '60s by a sister-in-law. It was altered by her daughter who worked in a bakery while attending college.

2½ cups warm water
2 tablespoons active dry yeast
3 tablespoons vegetable oil
½ cup packed brown sugar
3½ cups whole wheat flour
2 cups bread flour
2¼ teaspoons salt

❶ Spray 15x10x1-inch baking pan with nonstick cooking spray. In large bowl, combine warm water, yeast, oil, brown sugar, whole wheat flour, bread flour and salt; mix well. Knead mixture until dough is easy to handle; let rise. Shape dough into 24 buns. Cover, let rise in warm place, away from drafts, until doubled. Heat oven to 400°F. Arrange buns in pan. Bake 15 minutes or until golden brown.

2 dozen buns.

CRESCENT ROLLS

JOHN AND PAULA MOORE
LEECHBURG, PENNSYLVANIA

This recipe is from my grandmother. I make these rolls quite often for special occasions and holidays.

1 cup milk, scalded
½ cup shortening
½ cup sugar
1 teaspoon salt
1 (¼-oz.) pkg. active dry yeast
3 eggs, beaten
4½ cups all-purpose flour
    Melted butter, for brushing dough

❶ Spray 15x10x1-inch baking pan with nonstick cooking spray. In medium bowl, combine milk, shortening, sugar and salt; mix well. Add yeast; stir well. Add eggs and flour; mix to form soft dough. Knead. Cover; let rise in warm place, away from drafts, until doubled. Heat oven to 400°F.

❷ Divide dough into thirds. Roll each third into 9-inch circle. Cut each circle into 12 equal pieces; arrange on pan. Brush with butter. Cover; let rise until very light. Bake 15 minutes or until golden.

3 dozen rolls.

PERFECT POPOVERS

SUZANNE SROUJL
TEHACHAPI, CALIFORNIA

This was my grandmother's recipe, and her mother taught it to her. I've since passed it along to my two daughters. The popovers are just filling enough to keep tummies from rumbling at church on Sundays.

1 cup milk
1 tablespoon vegetable oil
2 eggs, beaten
1 cup all-purpose flour
¼ teaspoon salt

❶ Heat oven to 400°F. Spray 6 custard cups with nonstick cooking spray. Place custard cups on 15x10x1-inch baking pan.

❷ In medium bowl, stir milk, oil and eggs to mix well. Add flour and salt; whisk or beat at medium speed until smooth. Pour batter into cups, filling them half way. Bake about 40 minutes. Prick with fork immediately after baking.

6 popovers.

CUBAN BREAD

WILLIAM WEEDMAN, JR.
ALGOMA, WISCONSIN

Mom made this delicious crusty bread years ago and we loved it. The recipe was lost during a move but thankfully found.

1 (¼-oz.) pkg. active dry yeast
2 cups lukewarm water
1 tablespoon salt
1 tablespoon sugar
6 cups all-purpose flour
    Yellow cornmeal

❶ In large bowl, dissolve yeast in lukewarm water. Stir in salt and sugar. Add flour, 1 cup at a time, beating with wooden spoon until dough is smooth and well mixed. Cover; let rise in warm place, away from drafts, until doubled. Turn dough out onto lightly floured board; shape into 2 long French-style loaves.

❷ Sprinkle 15x10x1-inch baking pan with cornmeal; place loaves on pan. Let loaves rise 5 minutes. Slash tops of loaves crossways in 2 or 3 places with knife; brush each with water. Heat oven to 400°F. Place pan of hot water on bottom oven shelf; place loaves on shelf above. Bake 40 minutes or until golden.

2 loaves.

PILGRIM'S BREAD

BETTY PALMER
PARADISE, CALIFORNIA

This tasty bread recipe has been in our family for years.

½   cup yellow cornmeal
⅓   cup packed brown sugar
1   tablespoon salt
2   cups boiling water
¼   cup vegetable oil
2   (¼-oz.) pkg. active dry yeast
½   cup warm water (105°F to 115°F)
¾   cup whole wheat flour
½   cup rye flour
4   to 4½ cups all-purpose flour

❶ In medium bowl, combine cornmeal, brown sugar and salt. In another bowl, gradually stir mixture into boiling water; stir in oil. Cool mixture to lukewarm.

❷ Soften yeast in warm water; stir into cornmeal mixture. Add whole wheat and rye flours; mix well. Stir all-purpose flour into mixture by hand. Knead about 8 minutes. Place dough in large greased bowl. Cover; let rise in warm place, away from drafts, until doubled, about 1 hour. Punch down. Divide into 2 balls. Cover; let rest 10 minutes.

❸ Heat oven to 375°F. Shape dough; place in 2 (9x5-inch) loaf pans. Let rise in warm place, away from drafts, until doubled. Bake 45 minutes. Cover if tops brown too fast. Remove pans from oven; let rest 5 minutes. Remove loaves from pans to wire rack.

2 loaves.

CRUSTY FRENCH BREAD

BARBARA BARTOLOMEO
RADNOR, PENNSYLVANIA

Nothing smells as good as hot bread in the oven. If I bake this bread when my family is home, one loaf always disappears before dinner.

1   (¼-oz.) pkg. active dry yeast
2   cups warm water (105°F to 115°F)
6   cups all-purpose flour, sifted
2   tablespoons sugar
1   tablespoon salt
2   tablespoons shortening
    Cornmeal
1   egg white
1   tablespoon cold water

❶ In large bowl, stir yeast into warm water until dissolved. Stir in 3 cups of the flour, sugar, salt and shortening; beat at medium speed until smooth. Slowly beat in enough of remaining 3 cups flour to make stiff dough. Turn out onto lightly floured surface; knead 5 minutes or until smooth and elastic, adding only enough remaining flour to keep dough from sticking.

❷ Place dough in large greased bowl; turn to coat. Cover; let rise in warm place, away from drafts, until doubled, about 45 minutes. Punch down; knead 1 minute on lightly floured surface. Divide dough into 3 even pieces (dough will be sticky). Roll each piece into 12x9-inch rectangle. Roll up from short sides, jelly-roll fashion; tuck ends under.

❸ Spray 15x10x1-inch baking pan with nonstick cooking spray; sprinkle with cornmeal. Arrange loaves, seam-side down, 2 inches apart on pan; cover with clean kitchen towel. Let rise 30 minutes or until doubled. Make several evenly spaced diagonal cuts on top of each loaf. Heat oven to 400°F.

❹ In small bowl, beat egg white lightly with cold water. Brush mixture evenly over each loaf. Place pan of hot water on bottom oven shelf; place loaves on shelf above. Bake 30 minutes or until loaves are golden brown and sound hollow when tapped. Remove from pan; cool on wire racks.

3 loaves.

BABA'S BREAD

TOBEY WHITTIER
AUGUSTA, MAINE

This recipe was brought over from Poland by my mom in the early 20th century.

1   quart whole milk
1   (0.6-oz.) pkg. active dry yeast
2   tablespoons salt
1   tablespoon butter, melted
2   eggs, beaten
9½ cups all-purpose flour
2   cups raisins
2   teaspoons ground cloves
1   egg white
1   tablespoon cold water

❶ In large microwave-safe bowl, heat milk in microwave on High about 2 minutes. Whisk in yeast, salt, butter and eggs. Gradually add 3½ cups of the flour. (This will be a soupy mixture.) Cover; let rise in warm place, away from drafts, about 3 hours. Mix in raisins and cloves. Stir in remaining 6 cups flour. Knead until mixture is smooth and elastic, no more than 5 minutes.

❷ Place dough in large greased bowl. Cover; let rise in warm place, away from drafts, about 2 hours. Separate dough into thirds; knead 2 minutes more.

❸ Spray 2 (9x5-inch) loaf pans with nonstick cooking spray. Place one loaf in each pan.

❹ Heat oven to 400°F. In small bowl, combine egg white and cold water. Brush mixture evenly over top of loaves. Bake 5 minutes. Reduce heat to 350°F. Bake 45 to 55 minutes more. Remove loaves from pans immediately.

2 loaves.

HONEY MUSTARD BREAD

BARBARA NOWAKOWSI
NORTH TONAWANDA, NEW YORK

This recipe is for your buffet table. It's delicious and easy to make.

3   to 3½ cups all-purpose flour
½   cup quick cooking oats, plus ¼ cup for sprinkling
1   teaspoon salt
¼   cup honey
2   tablespoons Dijon mustard
2   tablespoons butter
1   (¼-oz.) pkg. fast-acting dry yeast
1   cup very warm water (120°F to 130°F)
1   egg
1   egg white, lightly beaten
1   tablespoon water

❶ In large bowl, combine 1½ cups of the flour, ½ cup oats, salt, honey, Dijon, butter and yeast; mix well. Add very warm water; beat at low speed 1 minute, scraping bowl frequently. Increase speed to medium 1 minute, scraping bowl frequently. Beat in egg. Stir in enough remaining flour, ½ cup at a time, until dough is easy to handle. Turn dough out onto lightly floured surface; knead about 10 minutes or until smooth and elastic.

❷ Place dough in large greased bowl; turn greased-side up. Cover; let rise in warm place, away from drafts, until doubled, about 1 hour. (Dough is ready if indentation remains when touched.) Punch down dough; shape into ball.

❸ Spray 9-inch pie plate with nonstick cooking spray. Press dough into and up sides of pie plate; flatten slightly.

❹ In small bowl, combine egg white and 1 tablespoon water; mix well. Brush mixture over loaf; sprinkle with ¼ cup oats. Cover; let rise in warm place, away from drafts, 45 to 60 minutes or until doubled. Heat oven to 375°F. Bake 35 minutes or until loaf sounds hollow when tapped and is deep golden brown. Remove from pie plate to wire rack; cool.

1 loaf.

HONEY MUSTARD BREAD

UNLEAVENED CHEESE BREAD

DIANNA BOWMAN
AKRON, OHIO

This recipe is good hot, warm or cold anytime of the year for any meal, snack or picnic!

¾ cup butter, softened
8 oz. cottage cheese, at room temperature
1 (8-oz.) pkg. cream cheese, softened
1 teaspoon salt
2 cups all-purpose flour
¼ cup freshly grated Parmesan cheese

❶ In large bowl, beat butter, cottage cheese, cream cheese and salt at medium speed until very creamy. Slowly add flour; beat until mixture holds together.

❷ Divide dough into 4 or 5 small balls; slightly flatten each ball onto plastic wrap or aluminum foil. Wrap each ball up; refrigerate until ready to roll out, about 30 minutes. Heat oven to 350°F. Spray 15x10x1-inch baking pan with nonstick cooking spray.

❸ Place 1 ball at a time on floured surface; roll each into ⅛-inch-thick circle. With floured knife, cut each circle into 8 pizza-shape triangles.

❹ Generously sprinkle each triangle with Parmesan. Roll triangles up from large end to point of each; arrange on baking sheet. Bake 25 to 30 minutes or until light brown.

8 servings.

CORN FRITTERS

MYRNA BOYDSTON
ASHLAND, OREGON

My mother used to fix these a lot, and they are good!

1 cup all-purpose flour
1 teaspoon salt
1 teaspoon baking powder
2 eggs
¼ cup milk
1 tablespoon shortening, melted, plus more for frying
1½ cups cooked whole kernel corn

❶ In medium bowl, combine flour, salt and baking powder. In another medium bowl, beat eggs and milk. Add shortening and corn to egg mixture. Lightly combine flour and egg mixtures. In large skillet, heat shortening to 365°F. Fry fritters, a few at a time, until brown, about 4 to 6 minutes.

15 to 20 fritters.

SWISS EGG BREAD

RONALD ROSS KENDALL
GALION, OHIO

This recipe won me The Best of Class and Best of Show awards at the 2000 Crawford County Fair.

2 cups milk
¼ cup butter
¼ cup water
2 (¼-oz.) pkg. active dry yeast
3 tablespoons sugar
1 tablespoon salt
2 eggs
6 to 7 cups all-purpose flour
2 egg yolks
2 tablespoons water
 Melted butter for brushing loaves

❶ In small pan, scald milk over medium-high heat. Add butter, water and yeast; set aside to proof.

❷ In large bowl, combine sugar, salt and eggs. When milk mixture cools, stir into sugar mixture. Add flour, 1 cup at a time, until it comes away from sides of bowl. Remove to well-floured surface; knead in remaining flour until smooth and elastic.

❸ Grease another large bowl. Place dough in bowl; turn to coat well. Cover; let rise in warm place, away from drafts, until doubled, about 1½ hours. Punch dough down; shape into 2 loaves. Arrange loaves on well-buttered 15x10x1-inch baking pan; let rise 1 hour. Heat oven to 400°F.

❹ In small bowl, combine egg yolks and water; mix well. Brush mixture over loaves. Bake 40 to 45 minutes. Remove loaves to wire rack; butter tops. Cover; let cool.

2 loaves.

ROCK RIVER THRESHEREE CORN BREAD

TAMI ZYLKA
BLUE BELL, PENNSYLVANIA

My maternal grandfather was involved in the Rock River Thresheree Association for over 40 years. As kids we always went to their annual Labor Day Weekend festival. The highlight of grinding the corn into cornmeal inspired this recipe.

1   cup all-purpose flour
1   cup yellow cornmeal
¼   cup sugar
4   teaspoons baking powder
½   teaspoon salt
1   cup milk
¼   cup shortening
1   egg
½   cup butter, softened
¼   cup honey

❶ Heat oven to 425°F. Spray 8-inch square pan with nonstick cooking spray.

❷ In large bowl, combine flour, cornmeal, sugar, baking powder and salt. Add milk, shortening and egg; beat at medium speed until fairly smooth, about 1 minute. Pour batter into pan. Bake 20 to 25 minutes.

❸ Meanwhile, in small bowl, combine butter and honey; drizzle over top of baked loaf.

1 loaf.

ZUCCHINI CORN BREAD

WILLIE PEARSON
HILLSBORO, TENNESSEE

I've been cooking this wonderful recipe for 55 years.

½   teaspoon salt
2½   cups grated zucchini
1   (8-oz.) container sour cream
4   eggs, beaten
1½   cups self-rising cornmeal
1   teaspoon sugar

❶ Heat oven to 350°F. Spray 8-inch square pan with nonstick cooking spray. In colander, sprinkle salt over zucchini; let sit 10 minutes. Squeeze all liquid from zucchini, reserving liquid.

❷ In medium bowl, combine sour cream, eggs, cornmeal, sugar, zucchini and reserved liquid; mix well. Pour batter into pan. Bake 45 to 60 minutes or until golden brown.

9 servings.

MEXICAN CORN BREAD

DIANE GULBENKIAN
MATAWAN, NEW JERSEY

This is a recipe my grandmother made for us whenever we visited her in Texas. As good cold as it is hot from the oven, it continues to be a favorite among friends.

¾   cup yellow cornmeal
¼   cup all-purpose flour
1   cup cream-style corn
1   small onion, chopped
½   teaspoon ground cumin
⅓   cup vegetable oil
2   eggs
1   cup (4 oz.) grated cheddar cheese
1   (4-oz.) can diced green chiles, undrained

❶ Heat oven to 450°F. Spray 13x9-inch pan with nonstick cooking spray.

❷ In large bowl, combine cornmeal, flour, corn, onion, cumin, oil, eggs, cheese and chiles; mix well. Pour batter into pan. Bake 20 minutes or until golden brown. Serve hot or at room temperature.

8 servings.

LEFSE

LEFSE

PEGI LEE
PRIOR LAKE, MINNESOTA

Making Lefse for the holidays is our family's favorite tradition. We make the potato balls the night before. The next day, we take turns rolling out lefse, baking it on the griddle and eating it.

8   medium russet potatoes, unpeeled
2   cups unbleached all-purpose flour
½   cup butter, melted
1   teaspoon salt

❶ Fill large pot ⅔ full of water; heat to a boil over medium-high heat. Boil potatoes until tender. Drain potatoes; cool slightly. Peel potatoes; press through potato ricer into large bowl. Cover bowl; refrigerate 1 hour.

❷ To riced potatoes, add flour, butter and salt; mix well. Form mixture into 12 to 15 palm-size balls. Refrigerate overnight in covered container.

❸ With floured rolling pin, roll out on well-floured pastry cloth to ¹⁄₁₆-inch thick. Place each Lefse on 500°F Lefse griddle (16-inch-wide griddle); turn over when lightly brown. Transfer to tea towel; cover. Serve with butter and sugar, jam or fresh cheese.

15 lefse.

PASKA (SLOVAK EASTER BREAD)

MARLENE TROUT
MEADVILLE, PENNSYLVANIA

Since my childhood, this recipe has been made every Easter. One loaf is kept for the family; the other is given to friends.

BASIC DOUGH
1   (6-oz.) fresh cake yeast
1   cup warm water
1   tablespoon plus ½ cup sugar
2   cups milk, at boiling point
½   cup butter
8   cups all-purpose flour
2   tablespoons salt
3   eggs

CHEESE DOUGH
½   cup milk
1   cup sugar
1   (6-oz.) fresh cake yeast
16   oz. dry cottage cheese
1   cup golden raisins
4   egg yolks
1   teaspoon salt
1   teaspoon grated lemon peel
1   teaspoon baking powder
3   cups all-purpose flour, sifted
1   egg yolk, lightly beaten

❶ For Basic Dough: In small bowl, combine 1 cake yeast, warm water and 1 tablespoon of the sugar; set aside 5 minutes. In large bowl, pour boiling milk over remaining ½ cup sugar and butter. Set aside until mixture is lukewarm. Sift flour, 1 cup at a time, into bowl. Add salt, eggs, yeast mixture and milk mixture; knead until dough is smooth and elastic. Cover; let rise in warm place, away from drafts, until doubled in size, about 2 hours. When dough has doubled, turn out onto lightly floured board; shape into fourths. Cover; let rest on board about 15 minutes. Lightly punch 1 part of dough around edge to elevate center.

❷ For Cheese Dough: In clean small bowl, combine ½ cup milk and sugar. Add 1 cake yeast; let stand 5 minutes. In medium bowl, stir cottage cheese with spoon until smooth. Add raisins and milk mixture; mix until well combined. Add 4 egg yolks, salt, lemon peel, baking powder and flour. Knead well. Set dough aside to rise until doubled, about 2 hours.

❸ Place Cheese Dough around elevated center of Basic Dough; lightly make an opening in center. Join edges of center with outside edges, pressing carefully to completely cover Cheese Dough. Place in 9-inch tube pan; let rise, covered, 30 minutes. Heat oven to 325°F. Just before baking, brush top with beaten egg yolk. Bake 10 minutes. Increase temperature to 350°F; bake additional 40 minutes.

4 paskas.

CHOCOLATE CHIP ZUCCHINI BREAD

LISA THORN
ST. JOHNSBURY, VERMONT

Here's a wonderful recipe to finish off the zucchini in the garden. It's moist and great for freezing.

3   eggs
1   cup vegetable oil
2   cups sugar
2   cups peeled, grated zucchini
1   tablespoon vanilla
3   cups all-purpose flour
1   tablespoon ground cinnamon
1   teaspoon salt
1   teaspoon baking soda
¼   teaspoon baking powder
1   (6-oz.) pkg. chocolate chips
1   cup walnuts

❶ Heat oven to 350°F. Spray 9x5-inch loaf pan with nonstick cooking spray.

❷ In medium bowl, beat eggs until light and foamy. Add oil, sugar, zucchini and vanilla; mix well.

❸ In another medium bowl, combine flour, cinnamon, salt, baking soda and baking powder; mix well. Combine mixtures; stir until well blended. Stir in chocolate chips and walnuts. Pour batter into pan. Bake 1 hour or until golden brown. Cool on wire rack.

1 loaf.

GREEK NEW YEAR'S BREAD

DONNA JEAN HALDANE
SILVER CREEK, NEW YORK

This recipe was given to me by my Greek friend; it's a big hit during the holidays.

2   (¼-oz.) pkg. active dry yeast
5½ to 6 cups all-purpose or bread flour
1   teaspoon grated lemon peel
1½ teaspoons anise seeds
1½ cups milk
6   tablespoons margarine
⅓   cup sugar
1   teaspoon salt
4   eggs
1   tablespoon water
2   tablespoons sesame seeds

❶ In large bowl, combine yeast, 2 cups of the flour, lemon peel and anise seeds. In medium pot, heat milk, margarine, sugar and salt over medium heat until warm. Add milk mixture to yeast mixture. Add 3 of the eggs; beat until well mixed. Stir in remaining flour, 1 cup at a time, until dough is moderately stiff. Turn out onto floured surface; knead until smooth. Shape dough into ball; place in large greased bowl. Let rise in warm place, away from drafts, until doubled, about 1½ hours.

❷ Heat oven to 350°F. Spray 9-inch round pan with nonstick cooking spray. Remove dough from bowl; punch down. Divide dough into thirds. Place ⅓ in pan; flatten. Repeat with second ⅓. Cut final ⅓ into 2 sections; roll each into 18-inch-long rope, then twist and seal ends. Place 1 rope on top of each loaf.

❸ In small bowl, beat remaining egg and water. Brush mixture over each loaf; sprinkle each with 1 tablespoon sesame seeds. Bake 25 to 30 minutes or until golden brown.

2 loaves.

GREEK NEW YEAR'S BREAD

PUMPKIN BREAD

MARY ANN GRIFFIN
EDGEWATER, FLORIDA

This recipe has been in my family for years. I've made it for Christmas the last 33 years.

⅔ cup shortening
2⅔ cups sugar
4 eggs
1 (15-oz.) can pumpkin
⅔ cup water
3⅓ cups all-purpose flour
2 teaspoons baking soda
1½ teaspoons salt
½ teaspoon baking powder
1 teaspoon ground cinnamon
1 teaspoon ground cloves
⅔ cup coarsely chopped nuts
⅔ cup raisins

❶ Heat oven to 350°F. Spray 2 (9x5-inch) loaf pans with nonstick cooking spray.

❷ In large bowl, beat shortening and sugar until light and fluffy. Add eggs, pumpkin and water. Blend in flour, baking soda, salt, baking powder, cinnamon and cloves; stir in nuts and raisins. Pour batter into pans. Bake 65 to 75 minutes or until toothpick inserted near center comes out clean.

1 loaf.

BUTTERFLY ROLLS

SANDRA BODENDIECK
ST. LOUIS, MISSOURI

This recipe was given to me by my 90-year-old mother-in-law five years after I married. We still make this recipe and serve it to friends and family.

1 (¼-oz.) pkg. active dry yeast
1 cup warm water (105° to 115°F)
½ cup sugar
3 eggs
¾ cup butter, melted
4 cups all-purpose flour, sifted

❶ In large bowl, combine yeast and water; let stand. In medium bowl, combine sugar and eggs; beat until thick. Beat in butter and yeast mixture; mix well. Add flour, 1 cup at a time; stir well. Cover; refrigerate 30 minutes. Heat oven to 350°F.

❷ Spray muffin cups with nonstick cooking spray. Roll dough ¼ inch thick on floured surface; shape into rolls. Place rolls in muffin cups. Let rise in warm place, away from drafts, until doubled. Bake 10 to 12 minutes.

About 2 dozen rolls.

WEST INDIAN COCONUT BREAD

ANITA COYNE
BONITA SPRINGS, FLORIDA

Here's a great bread for brunch.

4 cups all-purpose flour
2 cups sugar
2 teaspoons baking powder
1 teaspoon salt
1 teaspoon ground cinnamon
1 teaspoon ground nutmeg
7 oz. shredded coconut
1 cup milk
½ cup cream of coconut
2 tablespoons sour cream
2 teaspoons vanilla
4 eggs, beaten

❶ Heat oven to 350°F. Spray 2 (9x5-inch) loaf pans with nonstick cooking spray.

❷ In large bowl, combine flour, sugar, baking powder, salt, cinnamon, nutmeg, coconut, milk, cream of coconut, sour cream, vanilla and eggs; mix well. (Mixture will be thick.) Pour batter evenly into pans. Bake 1 hour or until golden brown.

2 loaves.

MOM'S DATE AND NUT BREAD

BRUCE GOLDSTEIN
SCARSDALE, NEW YORK

Mom always makes this recipe when we ask for it.

1   cup chopped pitted dates
¾   cup chopped walnuts or pecans
1½   teaspoons baking soda
½   teaspoon salt
¼   cup shortening
¾   cup boiling water
2   eggs, lightly beaten
½   teaspoon vanilla
1   cup sugar
1½   cups sifted all-purpose flour

❶ Heat oven to 350°F. Spray 9x5-inch loaf pan with nonstick cooking spray.

❷ In large bowl, combine dates, nuts, baking soda and salt. Add shortening and boiling water. Let mixture stand 15 minutes. Stir to blend.

❸ In medium bowl, combine eggs and vanilla. Stir in sugar and flour. Add nut mixture; mix well but do not overmix. Pour batter into pan. Bake 1 hour or until toothpick inserted near center comes out clean. Cool completely before removing from pan.

1 loaf.

MOCHA-ORANGE MARBLE BREAD

CAROLINE ROGGENBUCK
PULLMAN, WASHINGTON

This recipe is a must during the holidays because of its delectable taste and beautiful design.

7   to 7½ cups all-purpose flour
1   (¼-oz.) pkg. active dry yeast
1   to 1½ cups milk
½   cup orange juice
½   cup sugar
1   tablespoon grated orange peel
¼   cup butter
1   teaspoon salt
2   eggs
¼   cup unsweetened cocoa
2   tablespoons coffee

❶ In large bowl, combine 3 cups of the flour and yeast. In medium saucepan, heat milk, juice, sugar, orange peel, butter and salt to 125°F, stirring constantly. Pour milk mixture into flour mixture; mix well. Add eggs; beat at low speed about 1 minute. Increase speed to high; beat 3 minutes more. Add enough remaining flour to make soft dough. Turn dough onto floured surface; knead until smooth and elastic, about 6 minutes. Divide dough into thirds. Knead cocoa and coffee into one third; shape into ball. Shape remaining ⅔ dough into ball. Place each ball in lightly greased bowl, turning to grease tops. Cover; let rise in warm place, away from drafts, until doubled, about 1¼ hours. Punch white dough down. Cover; let rest 10 minutes.

❷ On lightly floured surface, roll white dough into 20x10-inch rectangle. Repeat process with mocha dough. Place mocha layer on top of white layer. Starting with long side, roll up jelly-roll fashion; press edges to seal. Cut roll into 20 slices; place in well-greased 20-inch tube pan (about 3 layers). Cover; let rise until nearly doubled, 30 to 40 minutes.

❸ Heat oven to 350°F. Bake 40 to 45 minutes or until lightly browned. Immediately remove from pan; cool on wire rack. Drizzle with glaze if desired.

1 loaf.

HARVEST CHOCOLATE LOAF

BEV NIRENBERG
THOUSAND OAKS, CALIFORNIA

This recipe is the most requested by my friends. I've made it for over 30 years and it's a must at my home for Christmas holidays.

BATTER
½   cup butter, softened
1   cup granulated sugar
2   eggs
1¾   cups all-purpose flour, sifted
1   teaspoon baking soda
1   teaspoon ground cinnamon
½   teaspoon salt
½   teaspoon ground nutmeg
¼   teaspoon ground ginger
¼   teaspoon ground cloves
¾   cup canned pumpkin
¾   cup chocolate chips
¾   cup chopped walnuts

GLAZE
½   cup powdered sugar
⅛   teaspoon ground cinnamon
⅛   teaspoon ground nutmeg
1   to 2 tablespoons milk

❶ Heat oven to 350°F. Spray 9x5-inch loaf pan with nonstick cooking spray.

❷ For Batter: In large bowl, beat butter until light. Gradually add granulated sugar, beating until fluffy. Blend in eggs. In another bowl, sift together flour, baking soda, 1 teaspoon cinnamon, salt, ½ teaspoon nutmeg, ginger and cloves. Add to butter mixture alternately with pumpkin. Stir in chocolate chips and ½ cup of the walnuts. Pour batter into pan. Sprinkle with remaining ¼ cup walnuts. Bake 65 to 75 minutes. Remove from pan to cool. When cool, drizzle with glaze.

❸ For Glaze: In medium bowl, combine powdered sugar, ⅛ teaspoon cinnamon and ⅛ teaspoon nutmeg. Blend in enough milk for glaze consistency.

1 loaf.

MAGGIE'S BANANA NUT BREAD

DAWN STARR
MT. MORRIS, MICHIGAN

This recipe comes from my Great-aunt Maggie. It's the best I've found!

1   cup granulated sugar
½   cup packed brown sugar
1   cup shortening
1   teaspoon vanilla
4   eggs
4   cups all-purpose flour
2   teaspoons baking soda
2   teaspoons baking powder
1   teaspoon salt
1   cup buttermilk
6   to 7 mashed bananas
2   cups chopped nuts

❶ Heat oven to 350°F. Spray 4 (9x5-inch) loaf pans with nonstick cooking spray.

❷ In large bowl, beat granulated sugar, brown sugar, shortening, vanilla and eggs until light and fluffy. Add flour, baking soda, baking powder, salt and buttermilk; mix well. Add bananas and nuts; mix well. Pour batter into pans. Bake 40 to 45 minutes or until golden brown. Cool on wire racks.

4 loaves.

DESSERTS

CREAMSICLE DELIGHT

CATHY YATES
CICERO, NEW YORK

All ages enjoy this cool salad — a perfect picnic side dish or refreshing dessert.

3   cups water
1   (3-oz.) pkg. orange gelatin
1   (3⅛-oz.) pkg. tapioca pudding mix
1   (3⅛-oz.) pkg. vanilla pudding mix
1   (11-oz.) can mandarin oranges, drained
1   (8-oz.) container frozen whipped topping, thawed

❶ In large saucepan, boil water. Add gelatin, tapioca and vanilla pudding mixes; mix well. Return to a boil; remove from heat to cool. When cool, fold in oranges and whipped topping. Refrigerate overnight. Serve in 6-cup mold or 1½-quart bowl.

6 servings.

PEACHES AND DUMPLINGS

JAN SENRICK
HUDSON, WISCONSIN

My mother used to make this for our family of seven. I have fond memories of this dessert, and now my three children and their families do too.

PEACHES
1   (29-oz.) can sliced peaches in syrup
1   cup water

DUMPLINGS
1½ cups all-purpose flour
2   teaspoons baking powder
3   tablespoons shortening
¾   cup milk

❶ In large pot, bring peaches and water to a boil. In large bowl, combine flour and baking powder; cut in shortening thoroughly so mixture looks like meal. Stir in milk. Drop batter by spoonfuls into boiling fruit. Cook uncovered 2 minutes. Cover; simmer 10 minutes or until dumplings are fluffy. Serve with vanilla ice cream and a sprinkling of cinnamon.

6 to 8 servings.

GIGGI'S SNOW PUDDING

STEPHANIE PRICE
YORK, MAINE

This is my grandmother's recipe, and it is one of my favorites.

PUDDING
1   (¼-oz.) envelope unflavored gelatin
¼   cup cold water
1   cup boiling water
¾   cup sugar
2   tablespoons lemon juice

TOPPING
1   cup milk, scalded
1   egg yolk
¼   cup sugar
½   teaspoon cornstarch
    Dash vanilla
    Dash salt

❶ For Pudding: In bowl, soak gelatin in cold water 5 minutes. Add boiling water and ¾ cup sugar; stir until dissolved. Add lemon juice; refrigerate until mixture begins to harden. Beat until spongy; refrigerate until set.

❷ Meanwhile, prepare Topping: In medium saucepan, beat together milk, egg yolk, ¼ cup sugar and cornstarch. Heat until thickened over medium heat, stirring constantly. Flavor with vanilla and salt.

6 servings.

CUSTARD-CARAMEL BREAD PUDDING

ROBERT LONGSTRETH
HONOLULU, HAWAII

This recipe is about 150 years old; it came from a friend in Boston who brought it to a potluck wedding. There were dozens of traditional family recipes served, and this one was my favorite.

2   cups milk
1   teaspoon vanilla
3   eggs, beaten
    Dash salt
1   cup packed dark brown sugar
3   slices buttered white bread, crusts removed

❶ Heat oven to 350°F. In large bowl, combine milk, vanilla, eggs and salt. Spread brown sugar into bottom of 1-quart casserole. Top brown sugar with bread. Pour milk mixture over bread; cover casserole. Place in shallow pan of water. Bake 1 hour. Serve warm.

4 servings.

CHARLOTTE RUSSE DE RASPBERRY

BARBARA NOWAKOWSKI
NORTH TONONWANDA, NEW YORK

This is a beautiful and delicious dessert.

CRUST
18 ladyfingers, halved lengthwise
¼   cup orange-flavored liqueur
⅔   cup water
2   (¼-oz.) envelopes unflavored gelatin
¼   cup granulated sugar
3   tablespoons lemon juice
1   (10-oz.) pkg. frozen raspberries in syrup, thawed
1   pint (2 cups) whipping cream, whipped

TOPPING
1   tablespoon butter
½   cup sliced almonds
2   tablespoons granulated sugar
½   cup whipping cream
2   tablespoons powdered sugar

❶ Butter 9-inch springform pan. For Crust: Sprinkle ladyfingers with liqueur; arrange around side and bottom of pan (cut sides facing center and top of pan).

❷ In small saucepan, combine water and gelatin; let stand 2 minutes to soften. Heat mixture over low heat until gelatin dissolves, stirring occasionally. Remove from heat. Stir in ¼ cup sugar, lemon juice and raspberries; beat with wire whisk until frothy. Refrigerate 15 minutes or just until mixture begins to thicken. Gently fold cooled raspberry mixture into whipped cream. Pour into pan lined with ladyfingers. Refrigerate 4 hours or until mixture has set. Heat oven to 350°F.

❸ For Topping: Place butter in 1-quart casserole; melt butter in oven 1 to 2 minutes. Add almonds; coat well with melted butter. Bake 8 to 10 minutes or until almonds are golden brown, stirring occasionally. Remove casserole from oven; add 2 tablespoons sugar. Stir to coat. Cool completely.

❹ In small bowl, beat ½ cup cream and powdered sugar at high speed until stiff peaks form. Garnish dessert with whipped cream and almonds. Store in refrigerator.

12 servings.

SUMMER FRUIT DISH

BRENDA BROOKS
SEAT PLEASANT, MARYLAND

This is my favorite dessert when I need something cool and light on those hot summer days.

2   cups fresh cut pineapple
1   cup fresh blueberries, plus more for garnish
1   cup fresh raspberries, plus more for garnish
1   cup sliced peaches
1   cup seedless grapes
1   cup sliced mango
3   cups Champagne or ginger ale
    Whipped cream

❶ In large serving dish, combine pineapple, blueberries, raspberries, peaches, grapes and mango; refrigerate 2 hours. Pour Champagne over fruit; refrigerate 2 hours more. Serve cold with whipped cream. Garnish with additional berries.

12 servings.

MOM'S GERMAN CHEESECAKE

DAWN STARR
MOUNT MORRIS, MICHIGAN

A German lady gave my mom this recipe many years ago but not before she swore her to secrecy. I found it, wrote it down and just had to share it with the Cooking Club.

CRUST
1¼ cups all-purpose flour
½ cup sugar
1 egg
½ teaspoon baking powder
½ cup butter

FILLING
5 (8-oz.) pkg. cream cheese, softened
6 eggs
1⅓ cups sugar
¼ cup lemon juice
Dash salt

TOPPING
2 cups sour cream
3 tablespoons sugar
1 teaspoon vanilla
Dash salt

❶ Heat oven to 375°F. For Crust: In large bowl, combine flour, ½ cup sugar, egg, baking powder and butter; mix well. Spread mixture into bottom of 9-inch springform pan. Bake 15 minutes. Remove from oven; cool.

❷ For Filling: In clean large bowl, combine cream cheese, 6 eggs, 1⅓ cups sugar, lemon juice and dash salt; beat at medium speed until smooth. Pour filling into crust. Reduce oven temperature to 350°F. Bake 1 hour or until cake is just set. Remove cheesecake from oven; cool.

❸ Meanwhile, prepare Topping: In medium bowl, combine sour cream, 3 tablespoons sugar, vanilla and dash salt; mix well. Pour over cheesecake.

❹ Increase oven temperature to 425°F. Bake cheesecake 5 minutes. Turn oven off; let cool in oven with door closed. Chill before serving.

12 servings.

RHUBARB TORTE DESSERT

IRENE EISELE
READING, MINNESOTA

My family enjoys this recipe and I hope you do too.

CRUST
1 cup butter, softened
2 cups all-purpose flour
2 tablespoons sugar
Dash salt

FILLING
6 egg yolks
1 cup cream
2 cups sugar
¼ teaspoon salt
5 cups sliced rhubarb
¼ cup all-purpose flour

MERINGUE
6 egg whites
2½ tablespoons cold water
¼ teaspoon cream of tartar
⅛ teaspoon salt
½ teaspoon vanilla
3 tablespoons plus ½ cup sugar

❶ Heat oven to 350°F. For Crust: In large bowl, combine butter, 2 cups flour, 2 tablespoons sugar and dash salt until mixture crumbles. Press mixture into 13x9-inch pan. Bake 10 minutes.

❷ For Filling: In clean large bowl, combine egg yolks, cream, 2 cups sugar, ¼ teaspoon salt, rhubarb and ¼ cup flour; mix well. Pour mixture into crust. Bake 40 minutes or until set.

❸ Meanwhile, prepare Merringue: In clean large bowl, beat egg whites and cold water until frothy. Add cream of tartar, ⅛ teaspoon salt and vanilla; beat until stiff. Add 3 tablespoons of the sugar; beat until stiff peaks form. Add remaining ½ cup sugar; beat until stiff. Pile onto filling, spreading all the way around edges of pan. Bake 15 minutes. Cut into squares.

16 servings.

RHUBARB TORTE DESSERT

PUMPKIN PECAN CHEESECAKE

TRICIA CARPENTER
CORINTH, NEW YORK

My mom gave me this recipe and I gave it to my daughter shortly after she married. This is a holiday favorite!

CRUST
½   cup pecans, finely chopped
2   tablespoons granulated sugar
1   cup gingersnap crumbs (about 20 cookies)
5   tablespoons butter, melted

FILLING
2   (8-oz.) pkg. cream cheese, at room temperature
⅔   cup packed brown sugar
1   cup canned pumpkin
½   cup sour cream, at room temperature
3   eggs, at room temperature
1½ teaspoons pumpkin pie spice
     Pecan halves (optional)
     Whipped cream (optional)

❶ Heat oven to 325°F. For Crust: In medium bowl, combine ½ cup pecans, granulated sugar, gingersnap crumbs and butter. Press mixture firmly into bottom of 9-inch springform pan. Bake 8 minutes or until toasted.

❷ For Filling: In large bowl, combine cream cheese, brown sugar, pumpkin and sour cream; mix well. Add eggs and pumpkin pie spice; mix until well blended. Pour into crust. Bake 45 minutes or until just set. Cool pan on wire rack. Garnish with pecan halves and whipped cream, if desired.

12 servings.

RASPBERRY SWIRL CHEESECAKE

DOUGLAS WAECHTER
CUBA CITY, WISCONSIN

This recipe is special because I made it for my wife's 35th birthday. It originated from a Valentine's Day present and my wife's passion for raspberries.

CRUST
1⅓ cups graham cracker crumbs
⅓   cup butter, melted

SAUCE
1   (10-oz.) pkg. frozen raspberries, thawed
¼   cup powdered sugar
2   teaspoons cornstarch

FILLING
3   (8-oz.) pkg. cream cheese, softened
¾   cup granulated sugar
2   tablespoons all-purpose flour
1   tablespoon vanilla
2   eggs
1   egg yolk
¼   cup heavy cream

❶ Heat oven to 375°F. For Crust: In medium bowl, combine cracker crumbs and butter. Press mixture evenly into bottom and 1 inch up sides of 9-inch springform pan. Wrap aluminum foil outside of and sides of pan; set aside.

❷ For Sauce: Press raspberries through sieve to remove seeds. Strain juice into medium saucepan. Stir in powdered sugar and cornstarch; stir over medium heat until thickened and bubbly. Reduce heat; stir 2 minutes. Remove from heat to cool.

❸ For Filling: In large bowl, beat cream cheese, granulated sugar, flour and vanilla at high speed until well mixed. Add eggs and egg yolk all at once. Reduce speed to low until combined. Stir in cream. Gently pour ½ of filling into crust. Pour in ½ of raspberry sauce. Pour remaining filling into crust; top with remaining raspberry sauce. With narrow spatula, swirl, being careful not to cut crust. Place pan in shallow pan on oven rack. Pour water into shallow pan. Bake 45 to 50 minutes or until nearly set.

❹ Remove pans from oven. Remove springform pan from shallow pan. Cool cheesecake in pan on wire rack 15 minutes. Use small metal spatula to loosen crust from pan sides. Cool 30 minutes; remove pan sides. Cool 1 hour. Cover; refrigerate 24 hours before cutting and serving.

10 to 12 servings.

CELEBRATION CRANBERRY CROWN CHEESECAKE

GWEN CAMPBELL
STERLING, VIRGINIA

I like to serve this festive and beautiful cheesecake on special occasions.

CRUST
3   tablespoons unsalted butter, melted
1   cup graham cracker crumbs
1   cup plus 1 tablespoon sugar

FILLING
½   cup chocolate chips
4   (8-oz.) pkg. cream cheese, at room temperature
1   cup sugar
2   tablespoons cornstarch
3   eggs
1   cup sour cream
1   teaspoon vanilla
6   tablespoons plus 1 teaspoon fresh lemon juice
1   tablespoon plus ½ teaspoon grated lemon peel
1   (16-oz.) can whole-berry cranberry sauce

❶ Heat oven to 325°F. Spray 9-inch springform pan with nonstick cooking spray. For Crust: In large bowl, combine butter, cracker crumbs and 1 cup plus 1 tablespoon sugar. Press mixture into bottom of pan. Chill.

❷ For Filling: Melt chocolate chips; set aside to cool. In large bowl, beat cream cheese, 1 cup sugar and cornstarch at medium speed until smooth. Add eggs, one at a time, beating well after each addition. Beat in sour cream and vanilla. Remove 2 cups of batter to bowl; beat in melted chocolate. Pour into pan; smooth top. Refrigerate. Stir 6 tablespoons of the lemon juice and 1 tablespoon of the lemon peel into remaining batter. Carefully spoon lemon batter over chocolate batter, smoothing top. Bake 1 hour 15 minutes to 1 hour 25 minutes or until knife inserted near center comes out just slightly moist. Cool completely; cover. Chill.

❸ Drain cranberry sauce; combine with remaining 1 teaspoon lemon juice and ½ teaspoon lemon peel. Spread over cheesecake. Refrigerate before and after cutting and serving.

10 to 12 servings.

PRALINE CHEESECAKE

REGINA ALBRIGHT
LAS VEGAS, NEVADA

This is my favorite dessert to serve at special dinners!

CRUST
1   cup graham cracker crumbs
¼   cup finely chopped pecans
⅓   cup butter or margarine, melted

FILLING
3   (8-oz.) pkg. cream cheese, softened
¾   cup packed brown sugar
3   eggs
2   teaspoons vanilla
    Whipped cream (optional)
    Chopped pecans (optional)

❶ Heat oven to 350°F. For Crust: In large bowl, combine cracker crumbs, ¼ cup pecans and butter; mix well. Press mixture into bottom and half way up sides of 9-inch springform pan. Bake 8 minutes. Set aside. Reduce oven temperature to 325°F.

❷ For Filling: In large bowl, beat cream cheese at high speed until creamy. Add brown sugar; beat well. Add eggs, one at a time, beating after each addition. Stir in vanilla. Pour mixture into crust. Bake 40 minutes. Turn oven off; leave cheesecake in oven with door partially open 30 minutes. Cool. Cover cheesecake; chill at least 8 hours. Remove from pan; top with whipped cream and pecans, if desired.

10 to 12 servings.

MARBLED PUMPKIN CHEESECAKE

MARBLED PUMPKIN CHEESECAKE

WAYEANN HYNEK
LUXEMBURG, WISCONSIN

I like to use this recipe on Thanksgiving because it's a little different from pumpkin pie.

CRUST
7   whole chocolate graham crackers, crushed
2   tablespoons plus 1 cup sugar
2   tablespoons butter, melted

FILLLING
¾   cup semisweet chocolate chips
3   (8-oz.) pkg. cream cheese, softened
1   tablespoon cornstarch
¾   teaspoon ground cinnamon
½   teaspoon ground ginger
⅛   teaspoon ground cloves
⅛   teaspoon ground nutmeg
1   teaspoon vanilla
2   eggs
2   egg whites
1   (15-oz.) can pumpkin

❶ Heat oven to 350°F. Spray 8-inch springform pan with nonstick cooking spray.

❷ For Crust: In small bowl, combine crushed crackers, 2 tablespoons of the sugar and butter until evenly moistened. Press into bottom of pan. Bake 8 minutes. Remove from oven; cool.

❸ For Filling: In small pot, melt chocolate chips over low heat; set aside. In large mixing bowl, beat cream cheese at high speed until smooth. Add remaining 1 cup sugar, cornstarch, cinnamon, ginger, cloves, nutmeg and vanilla. Reduce speed to medium; beat until well blended. Scrape bowl and beaters. Add eggs and egg whites; beat until mixed. Add pumpkin; beat at low speed until blended. Stir 2 cups pumpkin mixture into melted chocolate. Reserve ½ cup pumpkin mixture; pour remainder into crust. Pour chocolate mixture over pumpkin batter in crust in a thick ring, about ½ inch from sides. Top with dollops of reserved pumpkin batter; run knife through for marbled effect. Bake 1 hour 15 minutes or until toothpick inserted near center comes out clean.

❹ Remove pan from oven; run knife around edges. Cool cake in pan. Refrigerate, covered, at least 4 hours before removing sides of pan and serving.

12 servings.

OLD-FASHIONED CORNSTARCH PUDDING

BETTY PALMER
PARADISE, CALIFORNIA

My mother has made this pudding ever since I was a little girl and I still love it!

½   cup sugar
3   tablespoons cornstarch
¼   teaspoon salt
2   eggs, beaten
2¼   cups milk
1½   teaspoons vanilla or ¼ teaspoon almond extract
    Whipped cream or whipped topping

❶ In large saucepan, mix together sugar, cornstarch and salt.

❷ In small bowl, blend eggs and milk; gradually stir into saucepan. Cook over medium heat, stirring constantly. When thickened, boil 1 minute. Remove from heat; stir in vanilla. Pour into 6 oz. custard cups; chill. Top with whipped cream.

4 servings.

FLUFFY LEMON PUDDING

ROSE MOORE
CHESTER, ILLINOIS

The following recipe was one of my mother's favorites. It is wonderfully light after a heavy meal.

1   cup sugar
⅓   cup pastry flour or cake flour
    Grated peel and juice of 1½ lemons
1   cup milk
¼   cup cold water
2   eggs, separated
1   tablespoon butter, melted

❶ Heat oven to 350°F. Spray 1-quart casserole with nonstick cooking spray.

❷ In large bowl, combine sugar and flour. Add lemon peel, milk and cold water. Beat egg yolks; add yolks, butter and lemon juice to bowl.

❸ In medium bowl, beat egg whites to stiff peaks; gently stir into pudding. Pour into casserole. Bake 30 to 40 minutes.

6 servings.

MATTIE'S DATE PUDDING

VASHTI WILKINS
CABLE, OHIO

Mattie was a class mom to many girls at Enon, Ohio High School from 1937 to 1939. Her date pudding is the best I have ever tasted.

FILLING
1   cup all-purpose flour
1   cup packed brown sugar
1   cup chopped pitted dates
1   teaspoon baking powder
     Dash salt
½   cup milk

TOPPING
1   cup packed brown sugar
1   cup nuts
1   tablespoon butter
1   teaspoon vanilla
1¼   cups boiling water

❶ Heat oven to 350°F. Spray 9-inch square pan with nonstick cooking spray.

❷ For Filling: In large bowl, mix together flour, 1 cup brown sugar, dates, baking powder, salt and milk; pour into pan.

❸ For Topping: In clean large bowl, mix 1 cup brown sugar, nuts, butter, vanilla and boiling water; pour over filling. Bake 30 minutes.

9 servings.

GIGGI'S COFFEE JELLO

STEPHANIE PRICE
YORK, MAINE

My 91-year-old grandmother, affectionately called Giggi, always made this for family holiday gatherings.

1   (¼-oz.) envelope unflavored gelatin
½   cup cold water
1½   cups hot strong coffee
½   cup sugar
     Freshly whipped cream

❶ Soak gelatin in cold water 5 minutes. Add hot coffee and sugar; stir until dissolved. Pour mixture into 1-quart bowl; refrigerate until set. Serve with whipped cream.

6 servings.

BREAD PUDDING WITH SAUCE

JAMES PERRY
HOBBS, NEW MEXICO

This is a traditional recipe served at family gatherings. It is easy to fix, not too time consuming and travels well. It's a dish my grandmother asked for late at night.

PUDDING
4   cups half-and-half
6   eggs
½   to ¾ cup sugar, depending on preference
     Dash ground ginger
     Dash ground cinnamon
     Dash ground nutmeg
     Dash ground cardamom
     Dash ground cloves
     Dash ground mace
     Dash salt
     Dash freshly ground pepper
1   (1-lb.) loaf day-old bread, cubed, dried

SAUCE
1   (10-oz.) can coconut milk
¼   to ⅓ cup sugar, depending on preference
2   cardamom pods, crushed
1   (1- to 1½-inch) cinnamon stick
2   egg yolks, beaten
2   tablespoons rum (optional)

❶ For Pudding: Heat oven to 375°F. In large bowl, whisk half-and-half, eggs, sugar, ginger, ground cinnamon, nutmeg, ground cardamom, cloves, mace, salt and pepper until well mixed. Stir in bread cubes. Let sit at least 15 minutes to allow bread to absorb mixture; pour into 13x9-inch pan. Bake 45 minutes or until top is browned and pudding is set.

❷ For Sauce: In large saucepan, heat coconut milk, sugar, cardamom pods and cinnamon stick to a simmer. Remove from heat to cool; strain. Bring coconut milk mixture to a simmer again; remove from heat. Temper egg yolks by gently whisking in some of the coconut milk mixture until yolks reach same temperature as milk; pour back into saucepan with remaining milk. Cook over low heat until slightly thickened. Remove from heat; whisk in rum, if using. Strain, if desired. Serve over warm or room temperature pudding.

16 servings.

APPLE STRUDEL

RATZY NUSSBAUM
LAKEWOOD, NEW JERSEY

This recipe is a favorite from my mother's kitchen. Serve it hot, cold or at room temperature.

CRUST
1   egg
    Boiling water
3   cups all-purpose flour
2   tablespoons sugar
1   teaspoon baking powder
    Dash salt
½   cup vegetable oil

FILLING
    Vegetable oil
2   cups matzo meal
1   cup sugar, plus more for sprinkling
1   handful walnuts, ground (optional)
12 Cortland or Rome apples, sliced
2   tablespoons ground cinnamon
1   egg, beaten

❶ Heat oven to 350°F. Line baking sheet with parchment paper.

❷ For Crust: In measuring cup, beat egg and enough boiling water to make 1 cup, working quickly to prevent curdling. In large bowl, combine egg mixture, flour, 2 tablespoons sugar, baking powder, salt and ½ cup oil until dough forms; divide into fourths.

❸ For Filling: Roll dough, 1 piece at a time, to 17x15-inch rectangle; brush with oil. Sprinkle each rectangle with matzo, 1 cup sugar and walnuts, if using. Arrange ¼ of the apple slices in center of each dough; sprinkle with cinnamon. Fold dough over on both sides; seal edges. Place on large cookie sheet, seam-side down. Prick with fork; brush with beaten egg. Sprinkle with sugar. Bake 1 hour or until golden. When cool, slice. Place in oblong paper cupcake holders. Refrigerate.

About 24 servings.

RICOTTA BALLS DESSERT

DONNA VOALINO
CARBONDALE, PENNSYLVANIA

Many families from Sicily celebrate St. Joseph's Day on March 19th because many years ago there was a great famine. The people prayed to St. Joseph, but all that grew were chi chi beans. Every year we have a great St. Joseph's feast to remember this famine and, of course, we eat chi chi beans. This dessert recipe has become a tradition at our feast.

1   lb. ricotta cheese
¼   cup granulated sugar
2   eggs
2   cups all-purpose flour
2   teaspoons baking powder
1   teaspoon vanilla
    Vegetable oil
    Powdered sugar

❶ In large bowl, mix together ricotta, granulated sugar and eggs. Add flour, baking powder and vanilla; mix well.

❷ In Dutch oven, heat oil to 375°F. Drop batter by teaspoonfuls into oil; fry until brown. Cool ricotta balls; sprinkle with powdered sugar.

6 servings.

BLUEBERRY FRITTERS

EMMA VINCENT
GREENSBORO, NORTH CAROLINA

I always have to double the recipe when I make these because, in my household, they're gone by the end of the day.

2   tablespoons plus 1 cup all-purpose flour
1   cup fresh blueberries
¼   cup granulated sugar
2½ teaspoons baking powder
    Dash salt
½   cup milk
1   egg, beaten
    Vegetable oil
    Powdered sugar

❶ In medium bowl, combine 2 tablespoons of the flour and blueberries; toss lightly. Set aside.

❷ In another medium bowl, combine remaining 1 cup flour, granulated sugar, baking powder and salt; mix well. In small bowl, combine milk and egg. Gradually add milk mixture to flour mixture, stirring until smooth. Fold in blueberries.

❸ In Dutch oven, heat 3 to 4 inches of vegetable oil to 375°F. Drop 3 to 4 scant ¼ cupfuls of batter into oil at a time. Cook 3 minutes or until golden brown on 1 side. Turn; cook other side 3 minutes. Drain on paper towels; sprinkle with powdered sugar.

1 dozen fritters.

CRANBERRY CHEESE STRUDEL

CRANBERRY CHEESE STRUDEL

KIMBERLY ANTAL
LONGMEADOW, MASSACHUSETTS

It wouldn't be Christmas dinner without this — a wonderful ending to a special meal.

1   (12-oz.) pkg. cranberries, coarsely chopped
¾   cup plus 1 tablespoon granulated sugar
2   tablespoons cornstarch
½   teaspoon ground cinnamon
¼   teaspoon grated orange peel
¼   teaspoon grated lemon peel
⅛   teaspoon ground allspice
3   tablespoons water
1   (8-oz.) pkg. cream cheese, softened
¼   cup powdered sugar, plus more for sprinkling
½   teaspoon vanilla
15 sheets fresh phyllo dough
½   cup butter, melted
    Cornmeal

❶ In large saucepan, bring cranberries, granulated sugar, cornstarch, cinnamon, orange and lemon peels, allspice and 2 tablespoons of the water to a boil; boil gently 5 minutes, stirring frequently.

❷ Heat oven to 475°F. In large bowl, beat cream cheese, ¼ cup powdered sugar, remaining tablespoon water and vanilla until smooth. On sheet of parchment paper, carefully arrange 1 sheet of the phyllo into 18x14-inch rectangle. Brush with butter; sprinkle with 1 teaspoon cornmeal. Continue layering with 12 more sheets, brushing each sheet with butter and sprinkling alternate sheets with cornmeal. Spread cream cheese mixture evenly to within 1 inch from edges of top phyllo sheet. Continue layering 2 remaining phyllo sheets, butter and cornmeal.

❸ Starting 1 inch from short side, spread cranberry mixture evenly to cover ⅓ of phyllo rectangle, spreading mixture to within 1 inch from edges. From same short side of phyllo, roll up jelly-roll fashion. Place seam-side down on large ungreased baking sheet; brush with butter. Bake 40 to 45 minutes or until golden. When cool, sprinkle with powdered sugar. Serve with large dollops of freshly whipped cream or ice cream.

8 to 10 servings.

OLIEBOLLEN

NATASHA MILLARD
SURREY, BRITISH COLUMBIA, CANADA

This recipe is a Dutch New Year's Eve treat we have made on New Year's Eve Day every year for generations. Even now my sisters and I go to our parent's house on this special day to make this treat.

4   cups all-purpose flour
¼   cup sugar
2   tablespoons active dry yeast
1   teaspoon salt
2   cups warm milk
1   cup water
2   eggs, beaten
    Grated peel of 1 lemon
2   diced apples (optional)
1   tablespoon all-purpose flour (optional)
1   teaspoon ground cinnamon (optional)

❶ In large bowl, mix 4 cups flour, sugar, yeast and salt. In large microwave-safe bowl, combine warm milk, water, eggs and lemon peel. Microwave until lukewarm. Add milk mixture to flour mixture.

❷ This step is optional, but recommended: Add diced apples tossed with 1 tablespoon flour and cinnamon to batter. Put bowl of batter in oven alongside bowl of boiling water 45 to 60 minutes to let rise.

❸ Stir batter; fry spoonfuls of batter in deep fryer about 5 minutes, turning halfway through. Test first one to see if there is uncooked batter in the middle; adjust frying time accordingly. Best served warm, dipped in powdered sugar.

4 dozen balls.

BABA'S PAMPUSHKY

SHERRI PRICE
HILLTOP, MICHIGAN

Pampushky is a Ukranian dumpling with fruit filling, here with poppyseeds and prunes. Traditionally, they were served on Christmas Eve as part of the festivities. My Baba (grandmother) would make these year-round because she knew we enjoyed them so much.

CRUST
2   (¼-oz.) pkg. active dry yeast
¾   cup warm water (105°F to 115°F)
2   teaspoons plus 2 cups sugar
1   teaspoon salt
2½   cups warm milk
1   cup butter, melted
1   teaspoon lemon extract
1   teaspoon vanilla
8   egg yolks
4   eggs
4   to 5 cups all-purpose flour

POPPY SEED FILLING
1   to 1½ lb. ground poppy seeds
1   egg white, beaten
1   cup honey
¼   cup sugar
1   cup raisins

PRUNE FILLING
1   lb. dried plums (prunes)
½   cup sugar
1   tablespoon lemon juice
1   teaspoon ground cinnamon

❶ For Crust: In large bowl, mix together yeast, warm water and 2 teaspoons of the sugar; let sit 10 minutes. Add 2 cups sugar, salt, warm milk, butter, lemon extract, vanilla, egg yolks and eggs. Knead in enough flour to make smooth dough; knead until it no longer sticks to hands. (Dough should be soft but not sticky.) Cover; let rise in warm place, away from drafts, until doubled. Punch down; roll to ¼ inch thick. Cut out 2- to 2½ inch circles.

❷ For Fillings: In clean large bowl, mix together poppy seeds, egg white, honey, ¼ cup sugar and raisins. In large saucepan, cook dried plums in water until tender. Pit and chop dried plums. Add ½ cup sugar; cook until thickened. Add lemon juice and cinnamon. Place 1 teaspoon filling into center of each dough circle. Pinch ends together to seal. Roll in hands to form ball. Let rise until doubled. Fry in deep fryer at 350°F to 375°F until deep golden brown. Drain on paper towels or brown paper.

About 60 dumplings.

BAKLAVA

RITA HASHEMI
DUBLIN, OHIO

This recipe is an all-time favorite among family, friends and neighbors.

3   cups walnuts, finely chopped
2¼   cups sugar
1   tablespoon ground cinnamon
      Melted butter for brushing pan
12   sheets frozen phyllo dough (½ of 16-oz. pkg.), thawed
2   to 3 cups unsalted butter, melted
1   cup water
¼   cup honey
2   tablespoons lemon juice
½   teaspoon grated lemon peel
2   cinnamon sticks

❶ Heat oven to 325°F. In large bowl, combine walnuts, ¾ cup of the sugar and ground cinnamon. Brush bottom of broiler pan with melted butter. Stack ¼ of phyllo on pan, brushing each sheet generously with butter. Sprinkle with ⅓ of walnut filling. Repeat until all dough and filling is gone. With very sharp knife or pizza cutter, cut through layers to desired shape. Bake 45 minutes or until golden brown. Remove from oven; let cool completely.

❷ In large saucepan, bring remaining 1½ cups sugar, water, honey, lemon juice and peel and cinnamon sticks to a boil; simmer until thickened. Remove from heat; remove cinnamon sticks. Bring to room temperature; pour generously over Baklava. Although it may seem oversaturated, syrup will absorb and thicken with time. Cover with plastic wrap; store in refrigerator.

About 2 dozen servings.

CAKES & PIES

IRISH SCONES

MARGARET MAREAN
WISCASSET, MAINE

I received this recipe from a friend. I love making these scones as much as my family enjoys eating them; they're quick and easy when made in a food processor. The recipe is good with any dried and many fresh fruits.

2   cups all-purpose flour
2   tablespoons sugar
1   tablespoon baking powder
⅛   teaspoon salt
½   cup butter, cut up
½   cup raisins or any dried fruit, blueberries or other berries
½   cup cream
1   egg, beaten

❶ Heat oven to 425°F.

❷ In large bowl, combine flour, sugar, baking powder and salt. With pastry blender, cut in butter until mixture resembles cornmeal. Lightly stir in raisins.

❸ In small bowl, combine cream and egg; mix well. Add to flour mixture until dough forms; gently roll into ball.

❹ On lightly floured surface, knead dough a few times. Roll dough into ½-inch-thick round; cut into 12 equal wedges. Bake 15 to 20 minutes.

12 scones.

SPECIAL DAY COCONUT DEVIL'S FOOD CAKE

GWEN CAMPBELL
STERLING, VIRGINIA

My mother made this cake for my birthdays. It has always been a family favorite for special holidays.

CAKE
1   tablespoon plus ¾ cup unsweetened cocoa
⅔   cup boiling water
1¾   cups all-purpose flour
1¼   teaspoons baking soda
¼   teaspoon salt
¾   cup butter, at room temperature
1½   cups sugar
1   teaspoon vanilla
2   eggs
¾   cup buttermilk

COCONUT RUM FROSTING
2   egg whites
1   cup sugar
2   tablespoons water
⅛   teaspoon each salt, vanilla
¾   teaspoon plus 1 tablespoon dark rum or rum extract
1½   cups flaked coconut

❶ Heat oven to 350°F. Spray 2 (9-inch) round pans with nonstick cooking spray. Cut 2 (9-inch) circles from parchment paper; place in pans. Spray paper with nonstick cooking spray. Coat paper with 1 tablespoon of the cocoa.

❷ For Cake: In small bowl, combine remaining ¾ cup cocoa and boiling water; stir until smooth. Set aside. In medium bowl, combine flour, baking soda and ¼ teaspoon salt; mix well. In large mixing bowl, beat butter, 1½ cups sugar and 1 teaspoon vanilla at medium speed until light and fluffy. Add eggs, one at a time, beating well after each addition. Alternately add flour mixture and buttermilk to butter mixture, stirring just until smooth after each addition. Add cocoa mixture; blend thoroughly. Pour batter into pans. Bake 35 minutes or until toothpick inserted near center comes out clean. Cool in pans on wire rack.

❸ Meanwhile, prepare Frosting: In top of double boiler, combine egg whites, 1 cup sugar, water and ⅛ teaspoon salt. Place over simmering water; beat at medium speed with electric mixer until frosting holds its shape. Remove from heat; stir in ⅛ teaspoon vanilla and ¾ teaspoon of the rum. Place 1 cake layer on cake plate; brush with part of remaining tablespoon rum. Spread with 1 cup of the frosting. Place second layer over first; repeat procedure. Spread remaining frosting over top and sides of cake; press coconut over top and sides of cake.

12 servings.

ROSE'S GINGERBREAD

ROSELYN SHIVER
KNOXVILLE, TENNESSEE

I like gingerbread a lot because of the spicy taste. I added orange, almonds and dates to my batter and my friends are quite fond of it.

½ cup butter, softened
½ cup packed light brown sugar
½ cup light molasses
2 eggs
1½ cups all-purpose flour
½ teaspoon baking powder
½ teaspoon baking soda
¼ teaspoon salt
1 teaspoon ground ginger
1 teaspoon ground cinnamon
½ teaspoon ground nutmeg
¼ teaspoon ground cloves
½ cup orange juice concentrate
½ cup hot water
1 tablespoon finely grated orange peel
1½ cups sliced almonds
½ cup chopped black dates
¼ cup orange juice
2 tablespoons granulated sugar

❶ Heat oven to 350°F. Spray 2 (9x5-inch) loaf pans with nonstick cooking spray.

❷ In large bowl, beat butter, brown sugar, molasses and eggs until creamy. Mix in flour, baking powder, baking soda, salt, ginger, cinnamon, nutmeg and cloves until well blended. Add orange juice concentrate, hot water, orange peel, 1 cup of the almonds and dates; fold until evenly mixed.

❸ Spoon batter into pans. In small bowl, combine remaining ½ cup almonds and orange juice. Pour mixture evenly into pans; sprinkle with granulated sugar. Bake 40 to 45 minutes; cool on wire racks before removing from pans.

2 cakes.

OLD-FASHIONED GINGERBREAD

DONNA JEAN HALDANE
SILVER CREEK, NEW YORK

This recipe is over 100 years old and was passed on to me by my mother, Jane Lawrence.

½ cup shortening
½ cup sugar
1 egg
2½ cups all-purpose flour
1½ teaspoons baking soda
1 teaspoon ground ginger
1 teaspoon ground cinnamon
½ teaspoon salt
½ teaspoon ground cloves
1 cup molasses
1 cup hot water
Whipped cream (optional)

❶ Heat oven to 350°F. Spray 9-inch square pan with nonstick cooking spray; lightly flour.

❷ In large bowl, beat shortening, sugar and egg until light and fluffy. In another bowl, sift together flour, baking soda, ginger, cinnamon, salt and cloves. Mix molasses with hot water; add alternately with dry ingredients to shortening mixture. Beat well.

❸ Pour batter into pan. Bake 40 to 45 minutes. Serve with whipped cream, if desired.

16 servings.

POTATO SPICE CAKE
ETHELYN WELLES
BELLA VISTA, ARIZONA

My Grandmother made this holiday cake.

1   cup butter
2   cups granulated sugar
1   cup cold mashed potatoes
½   cup milk
4   eggs, lightly beaten
2   cups all-purpose flour
½   cup unsweetened cocoa
2   teaspoons baking powder
1   teaspoon ground cinnamon
1   teaspoon ground nutmeg
1   teaspoon ground allspice
1   teaspoon ground cloves
½   cup chopped pecans
    Powdered sugar
    Whipped cream (optional)
    Maraschino cherries (optional)

❶ Heat oven to 350°F. Spray 10-inch tube pan with nonstick cooking spray; lightly flour.

❷ In large bowl, beat butter and granulated sugar until light and fluffy. Add potatoes and milk; blend well. Add eggs, flour, cocoa, baking powder, cinnamon, nutmeg, allspice and cloves; blend thoroughly. Stir in pecans.

❸ Pour batter into pan. Bake 50 minutes or until toothpick inserted near center comes out clean. Remove pan from oven; cool. Remove cake from pan; dust lightly with powdered sugar. Garnish with whipped cream and cherries, if desired.

16 servings.

RAVANI (GREEK SPONGE CAKE)
CHARLOTTE WARD
HILTON HEAD ISLAND, SOUTH CAROLINA

This recipe was given to me by a friend who was an excellent cook and baker. She taught me a lot about Greek cooking and baking.

CAKE
6   eggs
1   cup farina (cream of wheat)
1   cup all-purpose flour
1   cup sugar
1   teaspoon orange juice
    Grated peel of 1 orange
2   teaspoons baking powder
1   cup butter, melted

SYRUP
2½ cups sugar
3   cups water
1   cinnamon stick
¼   teaspoon lemon juice
    Finely grated nuts or 6 cherries

❶ Heat oven to 350°F. Spray 13x9-inch pan with nonstick cooking spray.

❷ For Cake: In medium bowl, beat eggs until frothy. Add farina, flour, 1 cup sugar, orange juice, orange peel and baking powder; beat well. Slowly beat in butter. Pour batter into pan. Bake 25 to 30 minutes or until toothpick inserted near center comes out clean.

❸ Meanwhile, prepare Syrup: In medium saucepan, bring 2½ cups sugar, water and cinnamon stick to a boil over medium-high heat. Add lemon juice; simmer while cake is baking.

❹ When cake is cool, ladle some of the syrup over cake. Cut cake into 4 lengthwise sections. Pour more syrup over cake. Cut diagonally into 1½-inch diamonds; pour remaining syrup over cake. Sprinkle with nuts or place ½ cherry on each piece. Cover; refrigerate overnight.

12 servings.

RAVANI (GREEK SPONGE CAKE)

MARGARITA CAKE

MELISSA TOY
MEDFORD, NEW JERSEY

This is my favorite cake recipe.

½   cup water
1   orange, peel grated, halved, juice reserved
1¼ cups granulated sugar
3   tablespoons tequila
2   eggs
¼   cup nonfat milk
¾   cup all-purpose flour
1½ teaspoons baking powder
¼   cup butter, melted
     Powdered sugar (optional)
     Orange peel twists (optional)

❶ Heat oven to 375°F. Spray 9-inch springform pan with nonstick cooking spray.

❷ In small pan, combine water, orange juice, orange peel and granulated sugar; bring to a boil over medium-high heat until sugar has dissolved. Remove pan from heat; set aside. When cool, add tequila.

❸ In food processor, combine eggs, milk, flour, baking powder and butter; process until combined, scraping down container.

❹ Pour batter into pan. Bake 20 minutes or until cake pulls away from sides of pan and springs back when touched with finger. Pierce top of cake with fork in several places; slowly drizzle with tequila syrup. Remove pan sides, but not bottom. If desired, sprinkle cake with powdered sugar and decorate with orange twists.

8 servings.

HONEY CAKE

SHARI RAMSEY
ROCKFORD, ILLINOIS

This recipe came from my mother's kitchen; she's the best chef I know.

3½ cups all-purpose flour
1½ teaspoons baking powder
1   teaspoon baking soda
½   teaspoon ground ginger
½   teaspoon ground cinnamon
¼   teaspoon ground nutmeg
⅛   teaspoon ground cloves
3   eggs
¾   cup sugar
2   cups honey
¼   cup vegetable oil
¼   cup strong brewed coffee
¼   cup whiskey
1½ cups walnuts, chopped

❶ Heat oven to 325°F. Spray 2 (9x5-inch) loaf pans with nonstick cooking spray.

❷ In large bowl, sift together flour, baking powder, baking soda, ginger, cinnamon, nutmeg and cloves.

❸ In medium bowl, beat eggs and sugar until blended. Stir in honey, oil, coffee, whiskey and walnuts. Add to flour mixture; stir until blended.

❹ Pour batter into pans. Bake 45 minutes or until toothpick inserted near center comes out clean. Remove pan from oven to cool. Remove cake from pan when fully cooled.

16 servings.

TUTTI FRUITTI CAKE

SHIRLEY WILLIAMS
WAUPUN, WISCONSIN

This is my favorite birthday cake. My mother always made this for me, but only if I asked nicely.

CAKE
1   cup sugar
½   cup shortening
1   egg
1   teaspoon baking soda
1   cup buttermilk
1   (1-oz.) square chocolate, melted
1½ cups all-purpose flour
½   cup nuts
½   cup chopped pitted dates

FROSTING
½   cup sugar
½   cup milk
1   egg
½   cup nuts
2   tablespoons all-purpose flour
1   teaspoon vanilla

❶ Heat oven to 350°F. Spray 2 (9-inch) square pans with nonstick cooking spray.

❷ For Cake: In large bowl, beat 1 cup sugar, shortening and egg until light and fluffy. In measuring glass, combine baking soda and buttermilk. To bowl, add milk mixture, chocolate, 1½ cups flour, ½ cup nuts and dates; stir until combined.

❸ Pour batter into pans. Bake 35 to 40 minutes or until wooden pick inserted near center comes out clean.

❹ Meanwhile, prepare Frosting: In medium saucepan, boil ½ cup sugar, milk, egg, ½ cup nuts, 2 tablespoons flour and vanilla over medium-high heat until mixture is thick, stirring constantly. Spread frosting between cake layers. Assemble layers; frost cake.

24 servings.

SOUR CREAM POUND CAKE

WILLIE PEARSON
HILLSBORO, TENNESSEE

This is an old family recipe we've enjoyed over the years.

3   cups sugar
3   cups all-purpose flour
½   teaspoon salt
¼   teaspoon baking soda
1   cup butter
1   teaspoon vanilla
1   (8-oz.) container sour cream
6   eggs, beaten

❶ Heat oven to 350°F. Spray 10-inch tube pan with nonstick cooking spray.

❷ In large bowl, combine sugar, flour, salt, baking soda, butter, vanilla, sour cream and eggs; mix well.

❸ Pour batter into pan. Bake 1 hour or until toothpick inserted near center comes out clean.

16 servings.

SPICED CRANBERRY PEAR COBBLER

SPICED CRANBERRY PEAR COBBLER

KIMBERLY ANTAL
LONGMEADOW, MASSACHUSETTS

This recipe was acquired many years ago from an unknown source. I've reworked it over the years to reflect my tastes. It's perfect for a smaller holiday meal.

PASTRY
1¾ cups all-purpose flour
½ teaspoon salt
5 tablespoons chilled butter, cut into small pieces
⅓ cup chilled butter-flavored shortening
¼ cup ice water

FILLING
4 medium Bosc pears, peeled, cored and sliced lengthwise (¼ inch thick)
3½ cups cranberries
1¼ cups sugar, plus 1 teaspoon for dusting
¼ cup whole wheat flour
½ teaspoon ground allspice
¼ teaspoon ground cardamom
1 tablespoon butter

❶ For Pastry: In medium bowl, combine all-purpose flour and salt; add chilled butter and shortening. With pastry blender, combine until mixture resembles cornmeal. Sprinkle with ice water. Toss lightly with fork until dough holds together when pinched. Flatten dough to a round; wrap in plastic wrap. Refrigerate at least 30 minutes.

❷ Meanwhile, prepare Filling: In large bowl, combine pear slices and cranberries. Sprinkle with 1¼ cups sugar, whole wheat flour, allspice and cardamom; mix thoroughly. Spread fruit mixture into 13x9-inch pan; dot with 1 tablespoon butter. Heat oven to 375°F.

❸ On lightly floured surface, roll pastry to about ⅛ inch thick, making it 1 inch larger than rim of pan. Place pastry over fruit. Crimp border around rim. Cut 3 (2-inch) slits in pastry. Dust with 1 teaspoon sugar. Bake 45 minutes or until pastry is lightly browned and fruit is bubbling. Cool 15 to 20 minutes. Serve warm with vanilla ice cream.

6 servings.

HUMMINGBIRD CAKE

FANNIE KLINE
MILLERSBURG, OHIO

This is a very moist and beautiful three-layer cake that my family has enjoyed for years. It's wonderful for a fall family gathering when hiking and gathering nuts are events and baking is anticipated.

CAKE
3 cups all-purpose flour
2 cups granulated sugar
1 teaspoon baking soda
1 teaspoon salt
1 teaspoon ground cinnamon
1 cup vegetable oil
3 eggs, beaten
1½ teaspoons vanilla
1 (8-oz.) can crushed pineapple, undrained
2 cups chopped bananas
1 cup chopped pecans

FROSTING
1 (8-oz.) pkg. cream cheese, softened
½ cup butter, softened
4 cups powdered sugar
1 teaspoon vanilla
¼ teaspoon almond extract
½ cup chopped toasted pecans

❶ Heat oven to 350°F. Spray 3 (9-inch) square pans with nonstick cooking spray; lightly flour.

❷ For Cake: In large bowl, combine flour, granulated sugar, baking soda, salt and cinnamon. Add oil and eggs, stirring until dry ingredients are moistened. Stir in 1½ teaspoons vanilla, pineapple, bananas and 1 cup pecans. Pour batter into pans. Bake 25 to 35 minutes or until toothpick inserted near center comes out clean. Remove pans from oven; cool 5 minutes. Remove cakes from pans; cool on wire rack.

❸ Meanwhile, prepare Frosting: In medium bowl, blend cream cheese and butter until creamy. Add powdered sugar, 1 teaspoon vanilla, almond extract and toasted pecans; beat until smooth. Spread between cake layers. Assemble layers; frost cake.

12 servings.

NEW YEAR'S EVE ALMOND GOOD LUCK CAKE

VIVIAN NIKANOW
CHICAGO, ILLINOIS

I make this cake for every New Year's Eve dinner. One whole almond is baked into the cake and the person that finds it will have good luck the entire year.

CAKE
- 1 (2-oz.) pkg. slivered almonds, chopped
- ⅓ cup unsalted butter
- ⅓ cup shortening
- 3 eggs, separated
- 1¼ cups sugar
- 1 teaspoon grated lemon peel
- 2 tablespoons lemon juice
- 1 teaspoon vanilla
- 1 teaspoon almond extract
- 2⅓ cups sifted all-purpose flour
- 2 teaspoons baking powder
- 2 teaspoons baking soda
- ¾ teaspoon salt
- ¾ cup milk
- ½ teaspoon cream of tartar
- 1 whole almond

GLAZE
- ½ cup apricot preserves
- 1 tablespoon rum, triple sec or orange juice

❶ Heat oven to 350°F. Spray 12-cup Bundt pan with nonstick cooking spray. Sprinkle slivered almonds into pan; set aside.

❷ For Cake: In large bowl, beat butter, shortening and egg yolks, gradually adding 1 cup of the sugar, until light and fluffy. Add lemon peel, lemon juice, vanilla and almond extract; beat well. In medium bowl, combine flour, baking powder, baking soda and salt; mix well. Add to butter mixture alternately with milk, beginning and ending with dry ingredients, mixing well after each addition.

❸ In small bowl, beat egg whites and cream of tartar until foamy. Gradually add remaining ¼ cup sugar, beating until stiff peaks form. Fold whites into batter. Pour batter into pan. Press whole almond just below surface of batter. Bake 50 to 55 minutes or until toothpick inserted near center comes out clean. Remove pan from oven; cool 10 minutes. Remove cake from pan; cool completely.

❹ Meanwhile, prepare Glaze: Heat preserves in medium saucepan, then strain through sieve. Add rum; stir well. Drizzle over cooled cake.

16 servings.

RUM CAKE

SHARI RAMSEY
ROCKFORD, ILLINOIS

My mother used to make this cake for my dad and his buddies when they went deer hunting. I always knew a special mother-daughter weekend was ahead when I saw mom making it.

CAKE
- 1 cup chopped nuts
- 1 pkg. yellow cake mix with pudding
- 3 eggs
- ½ cup cold water
- ½ cup dark rum
- ⅓ cup vegetable oil

GLAZE
- ½ cup butter
- ½ cup water
- 1 cup sugar
- ½ cup dark rum

❶ Heat oven to 325°F. Spray 12-cup Bundt pan with nonstick cooking spray; lightly flour. Sprinkle nuts over bottom of pan.

❷ For Cake: In large bowl, combine cake mix, eggs, cold water, ½ cup rum and oil; mix well. Pour batter into pan. Bake 1 hour. Remove pan from oven; cool.

❸ Meanwhile, prepare Glaze: In medium saucepan, melt butter over medium-high heat. Stir in water and sugar; boil 5 minutes, stirring constantly. Remove from heat; stir in ½ cup rum.

❹ Remove cake from oven. Remove cake from pan; invert. Prick top of cake with toothpick. Spoon and brush glaze evenly over top and sides. Allow cake to absorb glaze.

16 servings.

CREAM CHEESE POUND CAKE

SUSAN WISNIEWSKI
GEORGETOWN, KENTUCKY

This is my mother's recipe, but I modified it to give it a lemon flavor. It is always popular among family at special gatherings.

CAKE
1½ cups butter, softened
1   (8-oz.) pkg. cream cheese, softened
6   eggs
3   cups granulated sugar
3   cups cake flour
1½ teaspoons vanilla

GLAZE
2   cups powdered sugar
3   to 5 tablespoons fresh lemon juice
2   teaspoons grated orange peel

❶ Spray 2 (9x5-inch) loaf pans with nonstick cooking spray.

❷ For Cake: In large bowl, beat butter and cream cheese until light and fluffy. Beat in eggs, one at a time. By hand, mix in granulated sugar, flour and vanilla. Pour batter into pans. Place in cold oven.

❸ Heat oven to 300°F. Bake 1½ hours or until toothpick inserted near center comes out clean. Remove pan from oven; cool cake in pan 10 minutes; remove to wire rack to cool.

❹ Meanwhile, prepare Glaze: In medium bowl, stir together powdered sugar and lemon juice, 1 tablespoon at a time, until glaze consistency forms. Stir in orange peel. Pour glaze evenly over warm cake. Let cool before serving.

16 servings.

ANISE SEED CAKE

LINDA ALBERTS
SUN PRAIRIE, WISCONSIN

This recipe is from my husband's Grandma Alberts. I added the anise flavoring and the cake has become a favorite of mine and my parents.

½   cup shortening
1   cup packed brown sugar
2   eggs
1   cup buttermilk
2   tablespoons molasses
2   cups all-purpose flour
1   teaspoon baking soda
½   teaspoon salt
½   teaspoon ground cinnamon
½   teaspoon ground allspice
½   teaspoon anise seeds
½   cup raisins

❶ Heat oven to 350°F. Spray 9x5-inch loaf pan with nonstick cooking spray.

❷ In large bowl, beat together shortening, brown sugar and eggs. Add buttermilk and molasses.

❸ In another large bowl, combine flour, baking soda, salt, cinnamon, allspice, anise seeds and raisins. Blend into shortening mixture.

❹ Pour batter into pan. Bake 45 to 60 minutes or until toothpick inserted near center comes out clean.

8 servings.

HOT FUDGE PUDDING CAKE

KAREN SWARTZ
ST. ALLEGAN, MICHIGAN

My family knows there won't be any leftovers with this chocolate dessert in the house.

CAKE
¾ cup granulated sugar
1 cup all-purpose flour
3 tablespoons unsweetened cocoa
2 teaspoons baking powder
¼ teaspoon salt
½ cup milk
⅓ cup butter, melted
1½ teaspoons vanilla

TOPPING
½ cup granulated sugar
½ cup packed brown sugar
¼ cup unsweetened cocoa
1¼ cups hot tap water

❶ Heat oven to 350°F.

❷ For Cake: In medium bowl, combine ¾ cup sugar, flour, 3 tablespoons cocoa, baking powder and salt. Blend in milk, butter and vanilla; beat at medium speed until smooth. Pour batter into 8-inch square pan.

❷ Meanwhile, prepare Topping: In small bowl, combine ½ cup sugar, brown sugar and ¼ cup cocoa; mix well. Sprinkle mixture evenly over batter. Pour hot water over top. Do not stir. Bake 40 minutes or until center is almost set. Remove from oven; cool 15 minutes before serving.

8 servings.

MY FAMOUS PUMPKIN ROLL

DARLENE LUKE
OKLAHOMA CITY, OKLAHOMA

My son requests this recipe instead of a cake on his birthday. Everyone who has tasted it has wanted the recipe. Now it's available to everyone. Enjoy!

CAKE
3 eggs
1 cup granulated sugar
⅔ cup canned pumpkin
1 teaspoon lemon juice
¾ cup all-purpose flour
2 teaspoons ground cinnamon
1 teaspoon ground ginger
1 teaspoon ground nutmeg
½ teaspoon salt
1 cup chopped pecans or walnuts
   Powdered sugar, for sprinkling

FROSTING
1 cup powdered sugar
1 (8-oz.) pkg. cream cheese, softened
2 teaspoons butter, softened
1 to 1½ teaspoons vanilla

❶ Heat oven to 375°F. Spray 15x10x1-inch baking pan with nonstick cooking spray.

❷ For Cake: In large bowl, beat eggs at high speed. Add granulated sugar, pumpkin and lemon juice. In another large bowl, stir together flour, cinnamon, ginger, nutmeg and salt. Fold in pumpkin mixture. Spread batter into pan; top with nuts. Bake 15 to 17 minutes; cool slightly. Turn cake onto towel; sprinkle with powdered sugar. Roll up towel and cake jelly-roll fashion. Cool in refrigerator.

❸ Meanwhile, prepare Frosting: In medium bowl, combine 1 cup powdered sugar, cream cheese, butter and vanilla; mix well. When roll is cool, unroll; remove towel. Smooth over flattened roll. Reroll. Slice to serve.

12 servings.

CHOCOLATE CHIP APPLE CAKE

CHERYL FULTON
NASHUA, NEW HAMPSHIRE

My mother-in-law made this dessert. I love it and share it with friends and family who also love it.

2 eggs, beaten
1 cup granulated sugar
¾ cup vegetable oil
1 cup chocolate chips
2 cups all-purpose flour
1 teaspoon baking soda
1 teaspoon ground cinnamon
¼ teaspoon salt
3 cups diced apples
2 teaspoons vanilla
½ cup nuts (optional)
   Powdered sugar (optional)

❶ Heat oven to 325°F. Spray 12-cup Bundt pan with nonstick cooking spray.

❷ In large bowl, combine eggs, granulated sugar, oil and chocolate chips; mix well. Stir in flour, baking soda, cinnamon and salt; mix well. Stir in apples and vanilla; mix well. Stir in nuts, if desired.

❸ Pour batter into pan. Bake 50 minutes or until toothpick inserted near center comes out clean. Remove pan from oven to cool. When cake is cool, invert onto serving platter. Sprinkle with powdered sugar, if desired.

14 servings.

PEANUT BUTTER TOFFEE PIE

WANDA MILLER
HARTFORD CITY, INDIANA

My mother usually made this pie during the holidays. I added the toffee bits last year and everyone loved it.

1 (9-inch) unbaked pastry crust
½ cup toffee bits
1 cup light corn syrup
⅓ cup peanut butter
½ cup sugar
3 eggs, lightly beaten
½ teaspoon vanilla

❶ Heat oven to 400°F. Place crust in 9-inch pie plate. Sprinkle toffee into bottom of crust.

❷ In large bowl, combine corn syrup, peanut butter, sugar, eggs and vanilla; mix well. Pour filling into crust. Bake 5 minutes. Reduce heat to 350°F; bake 30 to 40 minutes more.

8 servings.

GRANDMA'S BAKED TOPPING APPLESAUCE CAKE

MARILYN OTTOPAL
BLUE ASH, OHIO

This recipe, from my late mother-in-law, has been handed down from generation to generation.

CAKE
1 cup granulated sugar
1 cup packed light brown sugar
¾ cup shortening
2 eggs
2 cups applesauce
3 cups all-purpose flour
1 teaspoon baking soda
1 teaspoon baking powder
1 teaspoon salt
1 teaspoon ground cinnamon
1 teaspoon ground allspice
1 teaspoon ground nutmeg
½ cup raisins
½ cup chopped nuts

TOPPING
⅓ cup chopped pecans
⅓ cup sifted powdered sugar

❶ Heat oven to 350°F. Spray 10-inch tube pan with nonstick cooking spray; lightly flour.

❷ For Cake: In large bowl, beat granulated sugar, brown sugar and shortening until fluffy. Beat in eggs; add applesauce.

❸ In medium bowl, sift together flour, baking soda, baking powder, salt, cinnamon, allspice and nutmeg; mix well. Add to sugar mixture. Mix in raisins and nuts by hand.

❹ Meanwhile, prepare Topping: In small bowl, combine pecans and powdered sugar. Pour batter into pan. Sprinkle pecan mixture over batter. Bake 55 to 65 minutes or until toothpick inserted near center comes out clean. Cool in pan on wire rack.

12 servings.

FRUIT AND SPICE SHEET CAKE

BARBARA NOWAKOWSKI
NORTH TONAWANDA, NEW YORK

This cake is very delicious!

CAKE
2   cups all-purpose flour
2   teaspoons baking soda
2   teaspoons ground cinnamon
3   eggs
1½   cups granulated sugar
1   (28-oz.) jar mincemeat
½   cup vegetable oil
1   cup chopped nuts

FROSTING
¼   cup butter, softened
1   (3-oz.) pkg. cream cheese, softened
3   cups powdered sugar
1   teaspoon vanilla

❶ Heat oven to 350°F. Spray 15x10x1-inch baking pan with nonstick cooking spray.

❷ For Cake: In medium bowl, combine flour, baking soda and cinnamon; set aside. In large bowl, beat eggs and granulated sugar at medium speed until fluffy. Stir in mincemeat and oil. Add flour mixture and nuts; mix well. Turn batter into pan. Bake 35 to 40 minutes or until toothpick inserted near center comes out clean. Remove pan from oven; cool.

❸ Meanwhile, prepare Frosting: In clean medium bowl, beat butter and cream cheese until fluffy. Add powdered sugar and vanilla; mix well. Spread over cooled cake.

16 servings.

CLASSIC LEMON TART

LINDA MURRAY
ALLENTOWN, NEW HAMPSHIRE

This is a lovely tart for Easter (or any time). It's one of my husband's favorite treats.

CRUST
1¼   cups all-purpose flour
2   tablespoons sugar
½   teaspoon baking powder
¼   teaspoon salt
6   tablespoons shortening
¼   cup lukewarm milk

LEMON FILLING
2   eggs
3   egg whites
1   cup sugar
½   cup fresh lemon juice
2   teaspoons grated lemon peel
     Powdered sugar for dusting

❶ For Crust: In small bowl, combine flour, sugar, baking powder and salt. Cut in shortening with pastry blender. Pour in lukewarm milk; stir with fork to form soft dough. Wrap dough in plastic wrap; refrigerate 30 minutes.

❷ Heat oven to 375°F. Position rack in upper ⅓ of oven. Spray 9-inch pie plate with nonstick cooking spray.

❸ On lightly floured surface, roll dough into 12-inch circle. Drape dough over rolling pin to transfer to pie plate. Press into bottom and up sides to fit; trim edges. Cover crust with aluminum foil; weigh down. Place pie plate on baking sheet. Bake 10 to 12 minutes or until tart is set but not browned. Remove foil and weights; set pie plate on baking sheet aside.

❹ Meanwhile, prepare Filling: In large bowl, whisk eggs, egg whites and sugar until smooth. Slowly whisk in lemon juice and peel. Pour filling into partially baked crust. Bake tart in upper ⅓ of oven about 20 minutes or until crust is golden and filling is set. Cool on wire rack at least 10 minutes. Dust with powdered sugar. Serve warm, at room temperature or chilled.

8 servings.

CLASSIC LEMON TART

BEST EVER CARROT CAKE

TRICIA CARPENTER
CORINTH, NEW YORK

I spruce up this basic carrot cake recipe with walnuts, pineapple and coconut sprinkles. I make this whenever the family is in the mood, which is quite often.

CAKE
1½ cups corn oil
1¾ cups granulated sugar
3   eggs
2   cups all-purpose flour
2   teaspoons baking soda
½   teaspoon salt
1   tablespoon ground cinnamon
1   teaspoon ground cloves
2   cups grated carrots
1   cup chopped walnuts
1   (8-oz.) can crushed pineapple, drained

FROSTING
2   (8-oz.) pkg. cream cheese
1   cup powdered sugar
1   teaspoon vanilla

TOPPING
¾   cup shredded coconut

❶ Heat oven to 350°F. Spray 9-inch square pan with nonstick cooking spray.

❷ For Cake: In large bowl, beat oil, granulated sugar and eggs until well combined. In medium bowl, sift together flour, baking soda, salt, cinnamon and cloves. Add to oil mixture; mix well. Blend in carrots, walnuts and pineapple to mix well. Pour batter into pan. Bake 1 hour or until toothpick inserted near center comes out clean. Remove cake from oven; cool on wire rack.

❸ Meanwhile, prepare Frosting: In clean large bowl, beat together cream cheese, powdered sugar and vanilla. When cake has cooled, split into 2 layers; spread each with frosting. Reassemble cake. Sprinkle coconut evenly over top and sides.

8 servings.

PUMPKIN BREAD RING

THERESA STEWART
NEW OXFORD, PENNSYLVANIA

I've been making this recipe for about 25 years — it's especially delicious in the fall.

CAKE
3   cups buttermilk baking mix
1   cup granulated sugar
1   cup packed brown sugar
¼   cup butter
1   (15-oz.) can pumpkin
4   eggs
¼   cup milk
2   teaspoons ground cinnamon
½   teaspoon ground ginger
¼   teaspoon ground cloves
¼   teaspoon ground nutmeg

GLAZE
⅓   cup butter
2   cups powdered sugar
½   teaspoon vanilla
4   to 6 teaspoons hot water

❶ Heat oven to 350°F. Spray 12-cup Bundt pan with nonstick cooking spray; lightly flour.

❷ For Cake: In large bowl, combine baking mix, granulated sugar, brown sugar, ¼ cup butter, pumpkin, eggs, milk, cinnamon, ginger, cloves and nutmeg, Beat at low speed 30 seconds, scraping bowl constantly. Increase speed to medium; beat 3 minutes, scraping bowl occasionally.

❸ Pour batter into pan. Bake about 50 minutes or until toothpick inserted near center comes out clean. Cool cake in pan 10 minutes; remove from pan to cool completely.

❹ Meanwhile, prepare Glaze: In medium saucepan, heat ⅓ cup butter over medium heat until delicate brown. Blend in powdered sugar and vanilla. Stir in hot water, 1 teaspoon at a time, until smooth and of glaze consistency. Drizzle over cake.

16 servings.

CRANBERRY UPSIDE-DOWN CAKE

BEVERLY NIRENBERG
THOUSAND OAKS, CALIFORNIA

Here's a great alternative to the traditional pineapple upside-down cake. Its color is especially appealing during the Christmas holidays.

CRUST
1 cup butter
1 cup packed brown sugar
1 (12-oz.) pkg. fresh cranberries
½ cup chopped pecans

CAKE
1½ cups all-purpose flour
2 teaspoons baking powder
¼ teaspoon salt
1 cup granulated sugar
2 eggs, separated
1 teaspoon vanilla
⅓ cup milk

COGNAC WHIPPED CREAM
2 cups whipping cream
2½ tablespoons cognac
2 tablespoons granulated sugar

❶ Heat oven to 350°F. Spray 9-inch square pan with nonstick cooking spray. For Crust: Melt ½ cup of the butter in pan in oven. Remove pan from oven; stir in brown sugar. Spread evenly over bottom of pan. Arrange cranberries and pecans to cover bottom of pan.

❷ For Cake: In medium bowl stir together flour, baking powder and salt. In large bowl, beat 1 cup granulated sugar and remaining ½ cup butter at medium speed until fluffy. Add egg yolks and vanilla; beat at medium speed 1 minute, scraping bowl often. Add flour mixture alternately with milk to sugar mixture, starting and ending with flour mixture. Thoroughly wash beaters. In small bowl, beat egg whites at medium speed until soft peaks form; fold egg whites into batter. Spread batter over cranberries. Bake 35 to 40 minutes.

❸ Meanwhile, prepare Cream: In clean, large chilled bowl, combine cream, cognac and 2 tablespoons granulated sugar; beat with chilled beaters at medium speed until soft peaks form. Remove cake from oven. Cool pan on wire rack 10 minutes. Using knife, loosen edges of cake. Invert cake onto serving plate. Serve warm with Cognac Whipped Cream.

12 servings.

PUMPKIN RICOTTA CUSTARD PIE

LINDA MANIA
OCALA, FLORIDA

Here's a recipe for the most delicious pie I've ever tasted.

1 (9-inch) unbaked pastry crust
2 eggs, lightly beaten
1 cup ricotta cheese
1 (15-oz.) can pumpkin
1½ teaspoons apple pie spice
1½ teaspoons pumpkin pie spice
½ teaspoon salt
⅓ cup evaporated milk
 Vanilla ice cream (optional)

❶ Heat oven to 375°F. Place crust in 9-inch pie plate.

❷ In large bowl, combine eggs, ricotta, pumpkin, apple pie spice, pumpkin pie spice, salt and evaporated milk; blend well. Pour mixture into crust. Bake 1 hour or until toothpick inserted near center comes out clean. Refrigerate at least 1 hour before serving. Serve with ice cream, if desired.

8 servings.

DATE NUT APPLE CAKE

EARLENE BOLING
HUNTSVILLE, MISSOURI

This recipe is from my mother's recipe box. She always baked it on holidays. It's very moist and keeps well.

2 cups sugar, plus more for dusting
1 cup vegetable oil
1 teaspoon vanilla
3 eggs
2 cups all-purpose flour
1 teaspoon baking powder
½ teaspoon apple pie spice or ground cinnamon
1 cup chopped pecans
1 (12-oz.) pkg. finely chopped pitted dates
4 cups grated or finely chopped apples
 (Jonathon or Braeburn)
 Whipped cream (optional)

❶ Heat oven to 350°F. Spray 13x9-inch pan with nonstick cooking spray; lightly dust with sugar.

❷ In large bowl, combine 2 cups sugar, oil, vanilla and eggs; beat at medium speed until fluffy. Add flour, baking powder and apple pie spice; mix well. Add pecans, dates and apples; mix well.

❸ Pour batter into pan. Dust with sugar. Bake 1 hour. Remove cake from oven; cool. Serve with whipped cream, if desired.

12 servings.

RHUBARB CRUNCH

JOANNE DAEDA
HERMANTOWN, MINNESOTA

Once you've tasted this recipe, you too will be counting the days until fresh rhubarb comes up.

CRUST
1   cup all-purpose flour
1   cup packed brown sugar
¾   cup old-fashioned rolled oats
1   teaspoon ground cinnamon
½   cup butter, melted

TOPPING
4   cups diced rhubarb
1   cup granulated sugar
2   tablespoons cornstarch
1   cup water
1   teaspoon vanilla

❶ Heat oven to 350°F. Spray 9-inch square pan with nonstick cooking spray.

❷ For Crust: In large bowl, combine flour, brown sugar, oats, cinnamon and butter; mix until crumbled. Press half of the mixture into pan; cover with rhubarb.

❸ For Topping: In small saucepan combine granulated sugar, cornstarch, water and vanilla. Cook, stirring, until thick and clear. Pour over rhubarb. Top with remaining ½ crumb mixture. Bake 1 hour. Cut into squares; serve warm.

8 servings.

RHUBARB PIE

STEPHANIE PRICE
YORK, MAINE

Every summer we have a huge rhubarb patch and give a lot away to friends, neighbors and family. With what's left, I make this recipe from my mom's kitchen.

1   (9-inch) unbaked double-crust pastry
1⅓ to 2 cups sugar
⅓   cup all-purpose flour
4   cups cut-up rhubarb
1½ tablespoons butter

❶ Heat oven to 425°F. Spray 9-inch square pan with nonstick cooking spray. Place 1 of the pastry crusts in pan.

❷ In medium bowl, combine sugar, flour and rhubarb; mix lightly. Pour batter into pan; dot with butter. Cover with top crust. Cut slits in top; seal and flute. Cover edges with aluminum foil to prevent excessive browning. Bake 25 minutes; remove foil. Bake 20 to 25 minutes more or until crust is golden brown and juice begins to bubble through slits.

8 servings.

BLACKBERRY CREAM PIE

ELIZABETH McCONAHAY
NORFOLK, NEBRASKA

I took this pie to a teachers' party at Norfolk Junior High. It was subsequently featured in an all-school newsletter and requests followed!

1   (9-inch) unbaked pastry crust
1   cup plus 2 tablespoons sugar
1   cup sour cream
3   tablespoons all-purpose flour
¼   teaspoon salt
4   cups fresh blackberries or 1 (16-oz.) pkg. frozen, thawed
¼   cup fine dry bread crumbs
1   tablespoon butter, melted

❶ Heat oven to 375°F. Place crust in 9-inch pie plate.

❷ In medium bowl, stir together 1 cup of the sugar, sour cream, flour and salt. Place blackberries in crust; spread sour cream mixture over top.

❸ In clean medium bowl, combine bread crumbs, remaining 2 tablespoons sugar and butter; mix well. Sprinkle over top. Bake 40 to 45 minutes or until pie is golden brown.

8 servings.

APPELKUCHEN

KIMBERLY ANTAL
LONGMEADOW, PENNSYLVANIA

Friends are always asking for this dessert. It's an authentic traditional German recipe.

CRUST
2   cups all-purpose flour
½   cup unsalted butter, softened
½   cup sugar
1   teaspoon baking powder
    Dash salt
1   egg

FILLING
2   lb. apples (6 cups), cored, peeled and sliced
¼   cup sugar
¼   teaspoon ground cinnamon
½   cup sliced almonds
½   cup golden raisins

TOPPING
1   cup unsalted butter, cut into small pieces, thoroughly chilled
2   cups all-purpose flour
⅔   cup sugar
1   teaspoon ground cinnamon
¼   cup butter, melted
    Whipped cream

❶ Heat oven to 375°F. Spray 9-inch springform pan with nonstick cooking spray.

❷ In large bowl, combine 2 cups flour, softened butter, ½ cup sugar, baking powder, salt and egg; mix, kneading until supple dough forms. Roll dough to fit bottom of pan. Press dough into bottom and up sides of pan, patting to fit evenly.

❸ For Filling: Arrange apple slices on top of dough. Sprinkle with ¼ cup sugar, ¼ teaspoon cinnamon, almonds and raisins.

❹ Meanwhile, prepare Topping: In clean large bowl, combine chilled butter, 2 cups flour, ⅔ cup sugar and 1 teaspoon cinnamon with fingers or pastry blender. (It's best finished with fingertips). Spread mixture evenly over filling. Pour melted butter over crumb mixture. Bake 25 minutes. Reduce oven temperature to 350°F; bake 10 to 20 minutes more. (It may be necessary to loosely cover top of pan with aluminum foil to prevent excessive browning.) Remove pan from oven; cool to room temperature. Serve with whipped cream.

16 servings.

FROZEN PERSIMMON PIE

MARILYN KOVACH
ENCINITAS, CALIFORNIA

Over the years, I've come up with all kinds of persimmon recipes thanks to our lovely persimmon tree in the backyard. This is our favorite and it's usually served on Thanksgiving.

1   (9-inch) graham cracker crust
½   cup sugar
¼   teaspoon ground nutmeg
¼   teaspoon ground cinnamon
1   cup persimmon pulp, pureed
1   quart nonfat vanilla ice cream, slightly softened
¼   cup slivered almonds

❶ Place crust in 9-inch pie plate. In large bowl, combine sugar, nutmeg, cinnamon and pureed pulp; fold in ice cream. Turn mixture into crust; sprinkle with almonds. Freeze until firm, about 4 hours.

12 servings.

PEANUT BUTTER PIE

GLADYS LOVEJOY
WAUTOMA, WISCONSIN

When I was a waitress, I let the restaurant use my recipe for this pie. After retiring, people would call me for it because, no matter what, it just wasn't the same.

1   (8-oz.) pkg. cream cheese, softened
⅓   cup peanut butter
¾   cup sugar
2   tablespoons milk
2   cups whipped topping
1   (9-inch) graham cracker crust
¼   cup chocolate sprinkles

❶ In large bowl, combine cream cheese, peanut butter, sugar and milk. Fold in whipped topping. Pour mixture into crust; top with sprinkles. Pie can be frozen; thaw 30 minutes before serving.

8 servings.

BLUEBERRY PIE

VALERIE HOBBS
DEERFIELD, ILLINOIS

I have a ball making this recipe for my kids!

CRUST
2   cups all-purpose flour
2   teaspoons plus 2 cups sugar
¼   teaspoon salt
¾   cup shortening
⅓   cup finely chopped walnuts or pecans
1   teaspoon grated orange peel
5   tablespoons ice water

FILLING
2   pints (4 cups) blueberries
¼   cup cornstarch
½   teaspoon ground nutmeg

❶ For Crust: In large bowl, combine flour, 2 teaspoons of the sugar and salt. Cut in shortening with pastry blender. Add nuts, orange peel and ice water, 1 tablespoon at a time, mixing after each addition. Roll dough into ball; refrigerate 1 hour before using.

❷ Meanwhile, prepare Filling: In clean large bowl, combine blueberries, remaining 2 cups sugar, cornstarch and nutmeg. Remove dough from refrigerator; cut ball in half, then roll out. Press half of dough into 9-inch pie plate; fill with blueberry mixture. Top with remaining half rolled dough; slash top. Heat oven to 325°F. Bake 1 hour or until crust is brown and juice begins to bubble through slashes.

8 servings.

MOM'S REUNION BLUEBERRY PIE

TAMARA BANDSTRA
GRAND HAVEN, MICHIGAN

This is Mom's famous blueberry pie that we serve at every family gathering.

CRUST
4   cups all-purpose flour
1   lb. butter
1   cup sour cream
1   teaspoon vanilla

FILLING
2½   cups sugar
½   cup cornstarch
1   teaspoon salt
2¼   cups water
10   cups blueberries

❶ For Crust: In food processor, pulse flour and butter until consistency of small peas. Add sour cream and vanilla; process until just blended. Divide dough into 2 rounds; wrap each in plastic wrap. Refrigerate 2 hours.

❷ For Filling: In medium saucepan, combine sugar, cornstarch, salt and water over medium-high heat. Bring mixture to a boil; cook until thick, stirring constantly. Place blueberries in large bowl; pour hot sugar mixture over blueberries. Stir. Refrigerate mixture to cool.

❸ Heat oven to 325°F. Roll out 1 dough round; place in 15x10x1-inch baking pan. Spread cooled blueberry filling evenly to cover. Roll out remaining dough round; cover filling, crimping edges to seal. Bake 40 to 50 minutes or until crust is golden. Serve warm with vanilla ice cream.

16 servings.

PECAN TARTLETS

TAMI ZYLKA
BLUE BELL, PENNSYLVANIA

I wouldn't dare show up on Christmas Eve without these tartlets.

PASTRY
1   cup all-purpose flour
½   cup butter, softened
1   (3-oz.) pkg. cream cheese, softened
¼   teaspoon salt

FILLING
1   egg, lightly beaten
½   cup corn syrup
⅓   cup packed brown sugar
2   tablespoons butter, melted
1   teaspoon vanilla
    Dash salt
1   cup coarsely broken pecans
    Powdered sugar, for dusting

❶ Heat oven to 350°F. Spray miniature muffin cups with nonstick cooking spray.

❷ For Pastry: In large bowl, combine flour, softened butter, cream cheese and ¼ teaspoon salt; blend until dough forms ball. Divide dough into 24 equal pieces; roll into equal-size balls. Press into muffin cups, pressing dough up over edges of each cup.

❸ For Filling: In clean large bowl, combine egg, corn syrup, brown sugar, melted butter, vanilla and dash salt; blend well. Stir in pecans. Spoon mixture into pastry-lined cups. Bake 25 to 30 minutes or until filling is set but center is still soft; cool. Dust with powdered sugar.

24 tartlets.

CREAM CHEESE AND PECAN PIE

SUSAN WISNIEWSKI
GEORGETOWN, KENTUCKY

My mother-in-law gave me this recipe years ago. It's a family favorite and I think of her every time I make it.

PASTRY
1   (9-inch) unbaked pastry crust

FILLING
1   (8-oz.) pkg. cream cheese, softened
⅓   cup sugar
1   egg
¼   teaspoon vanilla
¼   teaspoon salt
1⅓   cups chopped pecans

TOPPING
3   eggs, beaten
¼   cup sugar
1   cup light corn syrup
1   teaspoon vanilla

❶ Heat oven to 375°F. Place crust in 9-inch pie plate.

❷ For Filling: In large bowl, combine cream cheese, ⅓ cup sugar, egg, ¼ teaspoon vanilla and salt; beat until thick and creamy. Pour mixture into crust; sprinkle with pecans.

❸ For Crust: In clean large bowl, combine 3 eggs, ¼ cup sugar, corn syrup and 1 teaspoon vanilla; mix well. Pour topping over filling. Bake about 40 minutes or until center is firm.

8 servings.

GREEN TOMATO PIE

JOANNE DAEDA
HERMANTOWN, MINNESOTA

Here's a great recipe for your green tomatoes in the fall!

1   (9-inch) unbaked double-crust pastry
3½   cups sliced green tomatoes
¾   cup raisins
1½   teaspoons grated lemon peel
½   teaspoon salt
2   tablespoons lemon juice
1   tablespoon cider vinegar
1½   cups sugar
3   tablespoons all-purpose flour
½   teaspoon ground cinnamon
⅛   teaspoon ground ginger
1   tablespoon dry bread crumbs
2   tablespoons butter

❶ Heat oven to 425°F. Place 1 of the crusts in 9-inch pie plate.

❷ In large bowl, combine tomatoes, raisins, lemon peel, salt, lemon juice and vinegar; mix well. In small bowl, blend together sugar, flour, cinnamon and ginger. Sprinkle bread crumbs evenly over crust; top with 2 tablespoons sugar mixture. Fold remaining sugar mixture into filling. Pour filling into crust; spread level. Dot with butter. Top with remaining crust. Poke steam holes with fork. Bake 15 minutes. Reduce heat to 350°F; bake 50 minutes more. Remove pie from oven; cool.

8 servings.

LEMON CUSTARD MERINGUE PIE

SHARON OBROCK
CHESTERFIELD, MISSOURI

I remember making my grandmother's pie with a miniature rolling pin, which I have today as a remembrance.

PASTRY
1   (9-inch) prepared pie crust

FILLING
2   cups granulated sugar
¼   cup cornstarch
     Juice of 2 lemons
¼   cup grated lemon peel
4   egg yolks, well beaten
2½   cups warm water
2   tablespoons butter

MERINGUE
2   egg whites, at room temperature
½   teaspoon cream of tartar
¼   cup powdered sugar
½   teaspoon vanilla

❶ Place crust in 9-inch pie plate.

❷ For Filling: In medium saucepan, combine granulated sugar, cornstarch, lemon juice, lemon peel and egg yolks. Pour warm water into mixture. Cook over medium heat, stirring constantly, until mixture thickens. Remove from heat; stir in butter. Pour mixture into crust. Heat oven to 350°F.

❸ For Meringue: In medium bowl, beat egg whites until frothy. Add cream of tartar; beat mixture until whites form stiff, soft peaks (not dry). Beat in powdered sugar, 1 tablespoon at a time. (Don't overbeat.) Beat in vanilla. Spread meringue over filling. Carefully seal along entire edge of crust to prevent shrinking. Bake 10 to 15 minutes or until golden. Remove pie from oven; cool on wire rack 2 hours. Refrigerate; serve cold.

8 servings.

COOKIES

BROWN EDGE WAFERS

CHARLOTTE WARD
HILTON HEAD ISLAND, SOUTH CAROLINA

This was one of my mother-in-law's favorite recipes and I plan on sharing it with my daughters and granddaughters. It's very delicious and very special.

½ cup butter
½ cup sugar
1 egg, beaten
¾ cup all-purpose flour
½ teaspoon salt
½ teaspoon vanilla

❶ Heat oven to 375°F. Line cookie sheet with parchment paper.

❷ In large bowl, combine butter, sugar, egg, flour, salt and vanilla; mix well. Arrange by small spoonfuls onto cookie sheet, about 9 spoonfuls per sheet. Bake 6 minutes.

About 2 dozen cookies.

SHORTBREAD COOKIES

DOLORES IOVINO
RIVERSIDE, ILLINOIS

This marvelous buttery cookie recipe was given to me by a colleague born in the United Kingdom.

3 cups all-purpose flour
1 lb. unsalted butter, softened
1 cup sugar
1 cup cornstarch

❶ In large bowl, combine flour, butter, sugar and cornstarch; mix well with hands until dough is a stiff heavy paste. Turn mixture into 13x9-inch pan; pat level. Prick with fork all over, making pattern on edge. Place pan in cold oven. Heat oven to 300°F. Bake 45 to 60 minutes or until lightly browned. Immediately cut into squares.

About 3 dozen cookies.

STAR LIGHT SUGAR CRISPS

BARBARA BRANDEL
OCALA, FLORIDA

My mother-in-law brought this recipe to the United States in 1914.

1 (6-oz.) pkg. fresh cake yeast
¼ cup warm water (105°F to 115°F)
3¾ cups all-purpose flour
1½ teaspoons salt
1 cup cold unsalted butter, cut up
2 eggs, beaten
½ cup sour cream
1 tablespoon vanilla
1½ cups sugar

❶ Dissolve yeast in warm water. In large bowl, combine flour and salt. With pastry blender, cut in butter until pea-size. Blend in yeast mixture, eggs, sour cream and 1 teaspoon of the vanilla; mix well. Cover; refrigerate 2 hours or up to 4 days.

❷ Heat oven to 375°F. In medium bowl, combine sugar and remaining 2 teaspoons vanilla. Sprinkle ½ cup sugar mixture over pasty cloth. Roll dough to 16x8-inch rectangle. Sprinkle about 2 tablespoons sugar mixture over dough.

❸ Fold dough into thirds; turn dough ¼ turn. Reroll dough; sprinkle with 2 tablespoons sugar mixture. Fold again into thirds; turn dough ¼ turn. Roll out; sprinkle with 2 tablespoons sugar mixture and fold. Add remaining sugar mixture to cloth or board as needed. For final roll: Roll dough to 16x8-inch rectangle, about ¼ inch thick. Cut into 4x1-inch strips. Twist each strip 2 or 3 times; place on ungreased cookie sheets. Bake 15 minutes.

About 64 cookies.

SWEET SUGARPLUM DREAMS
GWEN CAMPBELL
STERLING, VIRGINIA

These cookies have always meant a family get-together, whether after a light meal or at a midnight gab session with a cold glass of milk or cup of hot cocoa.

½   cup butter, at room temperature
¼   cup sugar
1   teaspoon vanilla
1¼ cups all-purpose flour
⅔   cup flaked coconut
½   cup hazelnuts, finely chopped
1   teaspoon grated orange peel
½   cup plum preserves

❶ Heat oven to 350°F. In large bowl, beat butter, sugar and vanilla until light and fluffy. Stir in flour, coconut, hazelnuts and orange peel until just combined. Form dough into tablespoon-size balls. With back of small spoon or your thumb, make indentation in each ball. Fill each with preserves. Arrange on ungreased cookie sheet. Bake 14 minutes or until lightly golden. Cool on cookie sheet 3 minutes before moving to wire rack. Cookies may be iced, glazed or sprinkled with powdered sugar.

1½ dozen cookies.

GINGERSNAPS
DAWN PAPE
MADISON, SOUTH DAKOTA

My grandmother used to make these cookies and I make them quite often for family.

1½ cups shortening
1   cup packed brown sugar
1   cup granulated sugar, plus more for coating
½   cup molasses
2   eggs
4   cups all-purpose flour
4   teaspoons baking soda
2   teaspoons ground cinnamon
1   teaspoon salt
1   teaspoon ground ginger
1   teaspoon ground cloves

❶ In large bowl, beat shortening, brown sugar, 1 cup granulated sugar, molasses and eggs until light and fluffy. Stir in flour, baking soda, cinnamon, salt, ginger and cloves. Refrigerate, covered, 1 hour. heat oven to 425°F. Roll dough into 1-inch balls. Roll balls in granulated sugar. Arrange on ungreased cookie sheet. Bake 8 minutes.

6 dozen cookies.

DRIED CRANBERRY AND ORANGE TEA CAKES
BARBARA NOWAKOWSKI
NORTH TONAWANDA, NEW YORK

I have been making these for a number of years. They are easy to make, delicious and will disappear in no time.

½   cup dried cranberries or raisins
1   teaspoon plus 2 cups all-purpose flour
¾   cup margarine or butter, softened
½   cup powdered sugar, plus more for sprinkling
1   egg
2   tablespoons sour cream
1   tablespoon grated orange peel
½   teaspoon orange extract
1   teaspoon baking soda
¼   teaspoon salt

❶ Heat oven to 325°F. In small bowl, toss cranberries and 1 teaspoon of the flour.

❷ In large bowl, beat margarine and ½ cup powdered sugar at medium speed until fluffy. Beat in egg, sour cream, orange peel and orange extract. Beat in remaining 2 cups flour, baking soda and salt at low speed. Stir in cranberries.

❸ Shape dough into 1-inch balls; arrange 1 inch apart on ungreased cookie sheets. Bake 12 to 15 minutes or until bottoms are lightly golden. Immediately remove from cookie sheets; cool slightly on wire rack. Sprinkle with powdered sugar.

3 dozen cookies.

COCOA SANDIES

MRS. P. D. HODGE
MADISONVILLE, TENNESSEE

These cookies make great holiday gifts for family and friends.

COOKIES
1   cup butter
1¼ cups powdered sugar, sifted
1½ teaspoons vanilla
½   cup unsweetened cocoa
1¾ cups all-purpose flour
¼   teaspoon salt

GLAZE
3   tablespoons butter
⅓   cup unsweetened cocoa
3   tablespoons water, plus more if needed
1   teaspoon vanilla
2¼ cups sifted powdered sugar

❶ Heat oven to 350°F. In large bowl, beat 1 cup butter, 1¼ cups powdered sugar and 1½ teaspoons vanilla at medium speed 3 minutes or until creamy. Add ½ cup cocoa; blend well, scraping sides often. Add flour and salt; beat until smooth, about 2 minutes.

❷ Roll dough on lightly floured surface to ½ inch thick. Using 2-inch heart-shaped cookie cutter, cut out 24 cookies. Arrange cookies on ungreased cookie sheet. Bake 15 to 20 minutes. Remove cookies from oven; cool.

❸ For Glaze: In small saucepan, melt 3 tablespoons butter over low heat. Stir in ⅓ cup cocoa and 3 tablespoons water, stirring constantly until thickened. Remove from heat; add 1 teaspoon vanilla. Gradually add 2¼ cups powdered sugar, whisking until smooth. Add more water, 1 teaspoon at a time, to achieve dipping consistency. Dip half of each heart into glaze leaving other half dry. Serve with fresh strawberries.

2 dozen cookies.

GOLDEN CARROT COOKIES

KAREN DAVIS
SAN JOSE, CALIFORNIA

This recipe is from my mother. These are wonderful eaten straight from the freezer in the summer.

COOKIES
1   cup shortening
¾   cup granulated sugar
1   cup mashed cooked carrots
2   eggs
2   cups all-purpose flour
2   teaspoons baking powder
½   teaspoon salt
¾   cup shredded coconut

FROSTING
1½ cups powdered sugar
2½ tablespoons butter, softened
1½ tablespoons orange juice
2   teaspoons grated orange peel

❶ Heat oven to 400°F. In large bowl, combine shortening, granulated sugar, carrots and eggs; mix well.

❷ For Cookies: In medium bowl, combine flour, baking powder and salt; mix well. Stir flour mixture into shortening mixture; stir in coconut. Drop dough by teaspoonfuls about 2 inches apart on lightly greased cookie sheet. Bake 8 to 10 minutes or until imprints remain when touched lightly.

❸ For Frosting: Sift powdered sugar into medium bowl; blend with butter. Stir in orange juice and peel until smooth. Frost warm cookies.

4 dozen cookies.

GOLDEN CARROT COOKIES

OATMEAL RAISIN COOKIES

RITA HASHEMI
DUBLIN, OHIO

This recipe is a tradition for every holiday in our house.

¾ cup butter
1 cup all-purpose flour
¾ cup granulated sugar
¾ cup packed brown sugar
2 eggs, at room temperature
1 tablespoon grated orange peel
1 teaspoon baking soda
½ teaspoon ground cinnamon
½ teaspoon ground nutmeg
1 teaspoon vanilla
2 cups old-fashioned rolled oats, ground
2 cups raisins
1 cup nuts, chopped

❶ Heat oven to 375°F. In large bowl, beat butter at medium speed until very soft. Add ½ cup of the flour, granulated sugar, brown sugar and eggs; mix well. Add orange peel, baking soda, cinnamon, nutmeg and vanilla; mix well. With large butter knife, add remaining ½ cup flour and oats; combine until dough is lumpy. Gently stir in raisins and nuts.

❷ Drop tablespoon-size dough onto ungreased cookie sheets. Bake 8 minutes for chewy cookies or 10 minutes for crunchy. Cool cookies on sheets 2 minutes. Place cookies on wire rack to cool completely.

4 dozen cookies.

PEPPERMINT-CHOCOLATE PUFFS

JUDY SAXBY
CONCORD, NEW HAMPSHIRE

This is my grandmother's recipe and my favorite cookie!

¾ cup butter
¾ cup sugar
1 egg, separated
1 teaspoon vanilla
2 cups all-purpose flour
½ cup crushed peppermint candies
54 semisweet chocolate chips

❶ Heat oven to 350°F. Spray cookie sheet with nonstick cooking spray.

❷ In large bowl, beat butter and ¼ cup of the sugar until light and fluffy; stir in egg yolk and vanilla. Gradually add flour, ¼ cup at a time. Stir in candies. Roll dough into 1-inch balls. Press 1 chocolate chip into center of each ball.

❸ In small bowl, lightly beat egg white. Dip balls into egg white; roll in remaining ½ cup sugar. Arrange balls on cookie sheet. Bake 15 minutes. Remove cookies from cookie sheet immediately; cool on wire rack.

4½ dozen cookies.

CHOCOLATE SPRITZ

TAMI ZYLKA
BLUE BELL, PENNSYLVANIA

Here's my family's favorite holiday cookie recipe.

½ cup sugar
¾ cup butter, softened
1 teaspoon almond extract
1 egg yolk
1½ cups all-purpose flour
¼ cup unsweetened cocoa

❶ Heat oven to 375°F. In large bowl, combine sugar, butter, almond extract and egg yolk; beat at medium speed until light and fluffy. Gradually add flour and cocoa until mixed. Place dough in cookie press. Form desired shapes on ungreased cookie sheet. Bake 7 to 9 minutes.

4 dozen cookies.

ZUCCHINI COOKIES

VERONICA HUNTER
ORLANDO, FLORIDA

*My Aunt Lucille made everything homemade, and this was
my favorite of her cookie recipes. I miss her when I make
them today.*

½ cup granulated sugar
½ cup packed brown sugar
½ cup shortening
2 eggs
1 cup shredded zucchini
1 teaspoon vanilla
2½ cups all-purpose flour
1 teaspoon baking soda
1 teaspoon ground cinnamon
½ teaspoon ground nutmeg
½ teaspoon ground cloves
¼ teaspoon salt
1 cup raisins
½ cup walnuts

❶ Heat oven to 325°F. In large bowl, beat granulated
sugar, brown sugar, shortening and eggs until light
and fluffy. Stir in zucchini and vanilla. In medium
bowl, combine flour, baking soda, cinnamon,
nutmeg, cloves and salt; add to zucchini mixture.
Mix in raisins and walnuts. Drop by spoonfuls
onto ungreased cookie sheets. Bake 15 minutes.

3 dozen cookies.

OLD-FASHIONED OATMEAL CHOCOLATE CHIP COOKIES

DONNA JEAN HALDANE
SILVER CREEK, NEW YORK

*Here's a World War II recipe my mother found. Since sugar
was rationed at the time, this became a family favorite.*

2½ cups all-purpose flour
2 cups packed brown sugar
1 teaspoon baking soda
½ teaspoon salt
1 cup butter
2 eggs
2 teaspoons vanilla
2 cups old-fashioned rolled oats
1 cup chocolate chips
½ cup chopped nuts

❶ Heat oven to 350°F. In large bowl, combine 1½
cups of the flour, brown sugar, baking soda, salt,
butter, eggs and vanilla; beat at medium speed
until well mixed. Add remaining 1 cup flour and
oats; beat 1 minute. Fold in chocolate chips and
nuts. Drop batter by teaspoonfuls onto ungreased
cookie sheets. Bake 10 to 15 minutes.

About 5 dozen (3-inch) cookies.

KIFFLES

MABEL CAMPBELL
AKRON, NEW YORK

*This is a recipe handed down by my mother. She made these
special treats for us every Easter and Christmas.*

3 eggs, separated
½ cup sugar
1⅓ cups butter, softened
⅓ cup shortening
3 cups all-purpose flour
⅔ cup sour cream
¾ cup ground walnuts
Powdered sugar, for dusting

❶ Heat oven to 350°F. In medium bowl, combine egg
yolks, sugar, butter and shortening; mix well. Stir
in flour and sour cream; mix well. Roll out dough
thinly; cut into 2-inch squares.

❷ In small bowl, beat egg whites well; stir in
walnuts. Spoon about ¼ teaspoon of mixture onto
each square. Fold opposite corners to center to
form triangles. Arrange about 1 inch apart on
greased cookie sheets. Bake 10 minutes; dust
cookies with powdered sugar.

6 dozen cookies.

RICKY'S FAVORITE BROWNIES

TOMMIE COULTER
FORNEY, TEXAS

Very simple. Very good. Ricky loves them.

½ cup butter
1 cup sugar
2 eggs, lightly beaten
2 (1-oz.) squares unsweetened chocolate, melted
1 teaspoon vanilla
½ cup all-purpose flour
½ cup chopped pecans or walnuts

❶ Heat oven to 325°F. Spray 8-inch square pan with
nonstick cooking spray.

❷ In large bowl, beat butter and sugar until light and
fluffy. Add eggs; beat until smooth and well
blended. Add chocolate, vanilla and flour; mix
well. Do not overbeat. Fold in nuts. Pour into pan.
Bake 35 minutes.

16 brownies.

PEPPERMINT BROWNIES

PEPPERMINT BROWNIES

ROSELYN SHIVER
KNOXVILLE, TENNESSEE

Here are my favorite (and very well liked) Christmas brownies.

BROWNIES
¾ cup butter, softened
2 cups sugar
4 eggs
1 teaspoon vanilla
1¼ cups all-purpose flour
1 teaspoon baking powder
½ teaspoon salt
½ cup Dutch-process cocoa
1½ cups miniature marshmallows
4 large peppermint patties, softened
½ cup chopped walnuts

FROSTING
1 cup chocolate chips
1 large peppermint patty
1 peppermint stick or 6 to 8 starlight mint candies, crushed

❶ Heat oven to 350°F. Spray 13x9-inch pan with nonstick cooking spray.

❷ For Brownies: In large bowl, combine butter, sugar, eggs and vanilla; beat until creamy. Add flour, baking powder and salt; mix well. Add cocoa, marshmallows and peppermint patties; beat at medium speed until creamy. Stir in walnuts. Spoon batter into pan. Bake 30 minutes or until set; cool.

❸ Meanwhile, prepare Frosting: In medium saucepan, melt chocolate chips and peppermint patty until smooth. Spread frosting over cooled brownies. Sprinkle crushed peppermints over brownies.

30 (1-inch) brownies.

ALMOND CAKE PASTRY

NATASHA MILLARD
SURREY, BRITISH COLUMBIA, CANADA

This is a traditional Dutch treat that my family enjoys at Christmas.

ALMOND PASTE
2 cups granulated sugar
4 eggs
Grated peel of 1 lemon
½ teaspoon almond extract

PASTRY
1 cup butter, plus more if pastry is dry
2 cups packed light brown sugar
2 eggs
3½ cups all-purpose flour
1 teaspoon baking soda
½ teaspoon baking powder
½ teaspoon salt
1 teaspoon almond extract

TOPPING
2 eggs
¼ cup milk
18 almonds, halved

❶ For Paste: In medium bowl, combine granulated sugar, 4 eggs, lemon peel and ½ teaspoon almond extract; mix well. Cover; refrigerate up to 1 week.

❷ For Pastry: In large bowl, combine butter, brown sugar, 2 eggs, flour, baking soda, baking powder, salt and 1 teaspoon almond extract; mix well. Roll out dough on floured surface. Using inverted glass, cut out cookies.

❸ Heat oven to 325°F. Place 1 cookie on ungreased cookie sheet; drop about 1 teaspoon almond paste in center. Top with another cookie; press edges together with fork. Repeat until all cookies are used.

❹ For Topping: In small bowl, whisk 2 eggs and milk until frothy; brush over cookies for shine. Press 1 almond half into center of each. Bake 20 to 25 minutes or until golden brown.

3 dozen (about 3¼-inch) cookies.

GUOKYA

MARIANNE HESTON
RALEIGH, NORTH CAROLINA

Here's a family recipe I remember making with my grandmother each Christmas. She made them with her mother in Italy. Now my mother and I make these cookies each year. It wouldn't be Christmas without them.

FILLING
1¼ lb. golden raisins
6   oz. almonds, toasted, ground
4   oz. walnuts, toasted, ground
4   oz. pecans, toasted, ground
4   oz. dried figs, chopped
1   to 2 oz. candied citrus fruit, chopped
¾   cup sugar
¾   teaspoon ground cinnamon
    Dash freshly ground pepper
½   cup dry red wine

PASTRY
2½ cups all-purpose flour
1   cup sugar
½   lb. shortening
½   cup warm water

TOPPING
3   egg whites, beaten
    Nonpareil sprinkles

❶ For Filling: In large pot, combine raisins, almonds, walnuts, pecans, figs, candied fruit, ¾ cup sugar, cinnamon, pepper, wine and enough water to cover. Bring to a slow boil over medium heat. Reduce heat to low; simmer, stirring often, 1 hour or until thick. Cover; refrigerate overnight.

❷ For Pastry: Heat oven to 350°F. In large bowl, with hands or pastry blender, blend flour, 1 cup sugar and shortening until dough resembles peas. Make well in center; add warm water, 1 tablespoon at a time, until ball of dough forms. Knead on work surface until surface comes clean, being careful not to add too much water; knead 5 minutes more. Shape into ball; cover with damp cloth. Working with ¼ dough at a time, roll out small circles large enough to make turnover cookie.

❸ For Topping: Spoon about 2 tablespoons filling into each center, folding dough over to make turnover; seal. Arrange on ungreased cookie sheets. Bake 10 minutes or until just beginning to brown. When done, arrange as many cookies as possible on baking sheet; brush with egg whites. Sprinkle with nonpareils; place under broiler a few moments to set egg whites.

50 cookies.

RAISIN LEBKUCHEN

KIMBERLY ANTAL
LONGMEADOW, MASSACHUSETTS

Growing up in Germany, I grew to love these sweet and spicy cookies. Over the years, I've developed my own version of this cookie to include my love of raisins.

½   cup packed light brown sugar
1   egg
1   cup honey
1   tablespoon grated lemon peel
1   teaspoon plus 1½ to 2 tablespoons lemon juice
2¾ cups all-purpose flour
1   teaspoon ground nutmeg
1   teaspoon ground cinnamon
1   teaspoon ground cloves
½   teaspoon baking soda
½   teaspoon salt
1   cup golden raisins
½   cup raisins
1   cup blanched slivered almonds, toasted
1   cup sifted powdered sugar

❶ Heat oven to 375°F. Spray 15x10x1-inch baking pan with nonstick cooking spray.

❷ In large bowl, beat brown sugar and egg until smooth and fluffy. Add honey, lemon peel and 1 teaspoon of the lemon juice; beat well. In medium bowl, sift together flour, nutmeg, cinnamon, cloves, baking soda and salt. Gradually add to brown sugar mixture at low speed. Stir in raisins and almonds. Spread batter into pan. Bake 18 to 20 minutes or until lightly browned; cool slightly.

❸ Meanwhile, in small bowl, combine powdered sugar with enough remaining lemon juice to make thin glaze; spread over bars. When thoroughly cool, cut into small rectangles.

3 dozen bars.

RAISIN LEBKUCHEN

DREAM BARS

IRENE EISELE
READING, MINNESOTA

I enjoy baking these delicious bars year-round.

BARS
1 cup butter
1 cup packed brown sugar
2 cups all-purpose flour

TOPPING
4 eggs, well beaten
2 cups packed brown sugar
2 teaspoons vanilla
½ cup all-purpose flour
1 teaspoon baking powder
½ teaspoon salt
3 cups shredded coconut
1½ cups chopped nuts

❶ Heat oven to 375°F. Spray 13x9-inch pan with nonstick cooking spray.

❷ For Bars: In large bowl, combine butter, 1 cup brown sugar and 2 cups flour until mixture crumbles. Pat mixture into pan. Bake 10 minutes; remove from oven.

❸ For Topping: In clean large bowl combine eggs, 2 cups brown sugar and vanilla. In medium bowl, combine ½ cup flour, baking powder, salt, coconut and nuts. Combine flour mixture and brown sugar mixture; stir well. Spread mixture over baked crust. Reduce oven temperature to 350°F. Bake 30 minutes or until brown. Cut into bars.

3 dozen bars.

MILK CHOCOLATE PEANUT BUTTER BARS

KARLA MEEHAN
CHAMPAIGN, ILLINOIS

My grandmother, along with her church group, made these bars every year for a Christmas bake sale.

BARS
⅔ cup butter, melted
¼ cup peanut butter
1 cup packed brown sugar
¼ cup light corn syrup
¼ teaspoon vanilla
4 cups quick cooking oats

TOPPING
1 cup milk chocolate chips
½ cup butterscotch chips
⅓ cup peanut butter

❶ Heat oven to 400°F. Spray 13x9-inch pan with nonstick cooking spray.

❷ For Bars: In large bowl, combine butter, ¼ cup peanut butter, brown sugar, corn syrup and vanilla; mix until blended. Gradually stir in oats. Press mixture into pan. Bake 12 to 14 minutes or until edges are golden brown. Cool on wire rack 5 minutes.

❸ Meanwhile, prepare Topping: In small saucepan, melt chocolate chips, butterscotch chips and ⅓ cup peanut butter over low heat. Stir until well blended. Spread over warm bars; cool completely. Refrigerate 2 to 3 hours before cutting.

4 dozen bars.

PEANUT BUTTER SQUARES

SHARON FLANAGAN
MISSISSAUGA, ONTARIO, CANADA

My friend and coworker, Jean Atkinson, passed this recipe on to me and now my family can't seem to do without them.

1½ cups peanut butter
1 cup butter or margarine
3½ cups powdered sugar
½ cup chocolate chips
16 peanuts

❶ In large bowl, combine 1 cup of the peanut butter and butter; mix well. Add powdered sugar; mix well. Spread mixture into 9-inch square pan. In small saucepan, melt remaining ½ cup peanut butter and chocolate chips over low heat; pour over mixture in pan. Refrigerate 1 hour or until set. Cut into squares; top each with 1 peanut.

16 squares.

MISSISSIPPI MUD BARS

RAMONA KLOPPING
OMAHA, NEBRASKA

This is my son's favorite bar. It's rich, delicious and easy to make.

BARS
1   cup butter
2   cups granulated sugar
4   eggs
¼   cup unsweetened cocoa
1½ cups all-purpose flour
¾   teaspoon salt
1   teaspoon vanilla
1½ cups pecans
1   (7-oz.) jar marshmallow crème

FROSTING
½   cup butter
⅓   cup evaporated milk
½   cup unsweetened cocoa
1   lb. powdered sugar
½   teaspoon vanilla
⅛   teaspoon salt

❶ Heat oven to 350°F. Spray 13x9-inch pan with nonstick cooking spray; lightly flour.

❷ For Bars: In medium bowl, beat 1 cup butter and granulated sugar until light and fluffy. Beat in eggs, one at a time. In medium bowl, sift together ¼ cup cocoa, flour and ¾ teaspoon salt. Add sifted ingredients to egg mixture. Stir in 1 teaspoon vanilla and pecans. Pour batter into pan. Bake 30 minutes. Remove pan from oven. Spread marshmallow crème over bars; let cool.

❸ Meanwhile, prepare Frosting: In large saucepan, bring ½ cup butter, evaporated milk and ½ cup cocoa just to a boil over medium-high heat. Add powdered sugar, ½ teaspoon vanilla and ⅛ teaspoon salt. Remove from heat; mix until fluffy. Spread over marshmallow crème.

3 dozen bars.

APPLESAUCE BARS

SANDRA BODENDIECK
ST. LOUIS, MISSOURI

My 90-year-old mother-in-law gave me this moist cake-like bar recipe. It is a family favorite.

BARS
¾   cup butter
1   cup granulated sugar
1   egg
2   cups all-purpose flour, sifted
2   teaspoons baking soda, sifted
1   teaspoon salt, sifted
½   teaspoon ground cinnamon, sifted
2   cups sweetened applesauce
1   cup raisins
1   cup nuts
1   teaspoon vanilla

FROSTING
½   cup butter
½   cup packed brown sugar
⅛   teaspoon salt
2   tablespoons cream or milk
½   cup powdered sugar
1   teaspoon vanilla

❶ Heat oven to 350°F. For Bars: In large bowl, beat ¾ cup butter and granulated sugar until light and fluffy; add egg. In medium bowl, combine flour, baking soda, sifted salt and cinnamon. Add alternately with applesauce, raisins, nuts and 1 teaspoon vanilla.

❷ Spread mixture into 15x10x1-inch baking pan. Bake 20 to 30 minutes or until golden brown.

❸ Meanwhile, prepare Frosting: In medium saucepan, melt ½ cup butter over medium heat. Stir in brown sugar and ⅛ teaspoon salt; boil 2 minutes. Add cream; boil 1 minute more. Add powdered sugar and 1 teaspoon vanilla. Spread mixture over warm bars.

4 dozen bars.

MOM'S APPLE SQUARES

STEPHANIE PRICE
YORK, MAINE

*My mom made these squares right after picking fresh apples.
They were a staple in our house every fall.*

3   eggs
1¾ cups sugar
2   cups all-purpose flour
1   teaspoon baking powder
½   teaspoon salt
1   teaspoon ground cinnamon
1   teaspoon vanilla
1   cup vegetable oil
2   cups peeled sliced apples
1   cup nuts
1   cup raisins

❶ Heat oven to 350°F. Spray 13x9-inch pan with
nonstick cooking spray.

❷ In medium bowl, beat eggs and sugar. Add flour,
baking powder and salt; mix well. Stir in
cinnamon and vanilla; blend in oil. Fold in apples,
nuts and raisins. Pour batter into pan. Bake 40
minutes or until cake bounces back when touched
in center.

3 dozen bars.

SWEET POTATO AND ORANGE BARS

BARBARA NOWAKOWSKI
NORTH TONAWANDA, NEW YORK

*Here's a favorite bar recipe I hope your family enjoys as
much as mine.*

BARS
1   cup butter, softened
1¾ cups packed brown sugar
1   cup all-purpose flour
½   cup sweetened condensed milk
1   teaspoon ground allspice
1   teaspoon ground cinnamon
¼   teaspoon salt
1   teaspoon orange extract
1   egg
1   (18-oz.) can vacuum-packed sweet potatoes,
    drained (1 cup)
¾   cup chopped pecans (optional)

FROSTING
½   cup light corn syrup
1   cup marshmallow crème
2   egg whites
½   teaspoon cream of tartar
¼   teaspoon ground cinnamon

❶ Heat oven to 350°F. Spray 13x9-inch pan with
nonstick cooking spray; lightly flour. For Bars: In
medium bowl, beat ¾ cup of the butter and ¾ cup
of the brown sugar at medium speed until fluffy.
Beat in flour at low speed. Press mixture into pan.
Bake 10 to 13 minutes or until light golden.

❷ In large bowl, beat remaining ¼ cup butter and 1
cup brown sugar at medium speed until fluffy.
Beat in sweetened condensed milk, allspice, 1
teaspoon cinnamon, salt, orange extract, egg and
potatoes at low speed until well blended. Pour
mixture over crust. Sprinkle with pecans, if using;
press lightly. Bake 29 to 33 minutes or until set.
Cool completely.

❸ Meanwhile, prepare Frosting: In small microwave-
safe bowl, microwave corn syrup, uncovered, on
High 1 to 2 minutes or until boiling. Stir in
marshmallow crème. In small bowl, beat egg
whites, cream of tartar and ¼ teaspoon cinnamon
at high speed until soft peaks form; beat in crème
mixture. Continue beating at medium speed until
stiff peaks form. Spread frosting over bars. Cut
into 2x1½-inch bars using hot, slightly damp knife.

3 dozen bars.

CHRISTMAS SCONES

KIMBERLY ANTAL
LONGMEADOW, MASSACHUSETTS

These fruit-studded scones have been a fixture of my holiday gift giving for years. They are wonderful for Christmas breakfast.

1½ cups all-purpose flour
¼ cup plus 1 tablespoon sugar
1½ teaspoons baking powder
½ teaspoon salt
½ cup butter, cut into pieces
¼ cup golden raisins, chopped
¼ cup dried cranberries
¼ cup plain yogurt or sour cream
¼ cup fresh orange juice
2 teaspoons grated orange peel
1 teaspoon ground cinnamon

❶ Heat oven to 425°F. Spray large baking sheet with nonstick cooking spray.

❷ In large bowl, thoroughly combine flour, ¼ cup of the sugar, baking powder and salt. With pastry blender, cut in butter until mixture crumbles. Stir in raisins, cranberries, yogurt, orange juice and peel until blended. Turn dough onto floured pastry board; roll to ¾ inch thick, shaping to neat circle. Cut into 8 to 10 wedges; place on baking sheet.

❸ In small cup, combine remaining tablespoon sugar and cinnamon; sprinkle over scones. Bake 10 to 12 minutes or until golden. Serve warm with butter.

8 to 10 scones.

GINNY'S FRUITCAKE

BECKY BENJAMIN
FOLSOM, CALIFORNIA

Here's my mom's fantastic fruitcake recipe. Every year she gets numerous requests for it.

1½ cups all-purpose flour
1½ cups sugar
1 teaspoon baking powder
1 teaspoon salt
5½ cups pecan halves, or mixture of pecans, walnuts, almonds and Brazil nuts
1 lb. diced candied pineapple
2 (16-oz.) cans maraschino cherries, drained
2 (7¼-oz.) pkg. pitted dates
6 eggs
⅓ cup rum
1 teaspoon vanilla
Rum or brandy

❶ Heat oven to 300°F. Spray 2 (9x5-inch) loaf pans with nonstick cooking spray; line with aluminum foil, allowing 2-inch overhang. Spray foil with nonstick cooking spray.

❷ In large bowl, sift together flour, sugar, baking powder and salt; add nuts, pineapple, cherries and dates; toss until coated. In small bowl, beat eggs and rum well; stir in vanilla. Pour over fruit mixture; mix until combined.

❸ Turn mixture into pans, pressing with metal spatula to pack tightly. Bake 1¾ hours or until toothpick inserted in center of loaf comes out clean. Cool loaves in pan 15 minutes. Remove from pans; peel off foil. Cool completely. Store in refrigerator.

2 loaves.

HOLIDAY FRUITCAKE

PAUL KRETZ
SAN FRANCISCO, CALIFORNIA

This is my maternal grandmother's recipe. It seems to please all fruitcake lovers. I remember looking forward to it on Thanksgiving and Christmas.

1½ cups seedless raisins
1½ cups dates, finely chopped
2   cups sugar
1   cup water
1   cup red wine
5   tablespoons shortening
3   cups all-purpose flour
1   teaspoon baking soda
1   teaspoon salt
1   teaspoon ground cinnamon
1   teaspoon ground cloves
1   cup candied fruit
1   cup chopped walnuts
     Whole candied cherries and walnut halves, for decoration

❶ Heat oven to 325°F. Spray 2 (9x5-inch) loaf pans with nonstick cooking spray; lightly flour.

❷ In large saucepan, simmer raisins, dates, sugar, water, wine and shortening about 10 minutes; let stand to cool. Add flour, baking soda, salt, cinnamon and cloves. Coat candied fruit and walnuts with a few spoonfuls of flour; add to mixture. Divide batter between pans. Decorate with candied cherries and walnut halves. Bake about 1½ hours (check at 1 hour 20 minutes) or until toothpick inserted in center of loaf comes out clean.

❸ When cool, wrap in plastic wrap and then aluminum foil. (The longer the loaves sit, the moister they become.)

2 loaves.

GRAMMY'S FUDGE

DEANNE ROBERTS
OREM, UTAH

My mom made this fudge every Christmas. It's still my favorite. The holidays wouldn't be the same without it in our home.

3   (8-oz.) pkg. semisweet chocolate squares, chopped
1   (13-oz.) jar marshmallow crème
2   tablespoons butter
1   teaspoon vanilla
4½ cups sugar
1   (12-oz.) can evaporated milk
2   to 3 cups chopped walnuts

❶ Line 13x9-inch pan with aluminum foil; spray with nonstick cooking spray.

❷ In large bowl, combine chocolate, marshmallow crème, butter and vanilla; mix well. Set aside.

❸ In large saucepan, mix sugar and evaporated milk. Bring to a boil over medium heat; boil 8 minutes, stirring constantly. Pour over chocolate mixture, stirring until chocolate is melted and ingredients are blended. Stir in walnuts. Pour into pan; refrigerate to cool. Cut into 1-inch squares.

4 lb.

CANDIED CHERRY ROCKY ROAD FUDGE

DIANA BAKER WOODALL
COTATI, CALIFORNIA

I started giving this recipe to family, friends and neighbors a few years back. They always ask me to make more!

2   cups semisweet chocolate chips
1   (14-oz.) can sweetened condensed milk (1¼ cups)
2   teaspoons maraschino cherry juice
1   teaspoon vanilla
½   teaspoon vanilla-nut flavoring (optional)
½   teaspoon coffee extract or flavoring
3   cups miniature marshmallows
1   cup candied cherries, halved
1½ cups coarsely chopped walnuts (optional)

❶ Line 13x9-inch pan with aluminum foil; spray foil with nonstick cooking spray. Or, to make small portions to give as gifts, use 3 or 4 small decorated foil baking tins with clear plastic lids.

❷ In large microwave-safe bowl, microwave chocolate chips and sweetened condensed milk on High 1 minute; stir. Microwave in 15 to 20 second intervals, stirring until smooth, until chocolate is melted. Stir in cherry juice, vanilla, vanilla-nut flavoring, if using, and coffee extract. Stir in marshmallows, cherries and walnuts, if using.

❸ Press mixture into pan or foil tins. Refrigerate until ready to serve, at least 1 hour. Lift fudge from pan; remove foil. Cut into pieces. (If making in foil tins, do not use foil to line tins; leave fudge uncut. Put clear plastic lids on tins.)

4 dozen.

BUTTERY CHOCOLATE NUT TOFFEE

NANCY WESTERGOM
WESTMONT, NEW JERSEY

This is one of my favorite treats to give to a dinner host or just to brighten someone's day. Everyone always loves and raves about this toffee.

1   cup sugar
1   cup butter
1   (16-oz.) pkg. semisweet chocolate chips
¼   cup walnuts

❶ In 2-quart saucepan, combine sugar and butter. Cook over low heat, stirring occasionally, until candy thermometer reaches 300°F or small amount of mixture dropped into ice water forms brittle strands, 25 to 30 minutes.

❷ Spread mixture on 15x10x1-inch baking pan lined with parchment paper. Sprinkle chocolate chips over hot candy; let stand 5 minutes.

❸ Spread melted chocolate evenly over candy; sprinkle with walnuts. Cool completely; break into pieces.

1¼ lb.

BUTTERY CHOCOLATE NUT TOFFEE

OPERA FUDGE

KAREN MARTIN
BOYERTOWN, PENNSYLVANIA

This is a delicious candy recipe I remember from my childhood in the Lebanon County area of Pennsylvania.

FILLING
½   cup butter
4   cups sugar
1   pint (2 cups) heavy whipping cream

CHOCOLATE COATING
1½ cups chocolate chips
2   tablespoons shortening

❶ For Filling: In 4-quart pot, melt butter over low heat. Stir in sugar and cream. Simmer until mixture reaches 240°F on candy thermometer. Do not stir while cooking. Cover; cool in pot.

❷ Line 13x9-inch pan with nonstick cooking spray. Pour filling into large bowl; beat at high speed until creamy. Pour into pan; freeze. When frozen, cut into squares; coat with chocolate coating.

❸ For Coating: In top of double boiler set over simmering water, melt chocolate chips and shortening.

150 small pieces.

PEANUT BUTTER FUDGE

AMELIA MOODY
PASADENA, TEXAS

This is an old country recipe from one of my neighbors back home. We make it at Christmas and it goes in a hurry! The recipe is nearly 100 years old.

26 marshmallows, cut into fourths
1½ cups granulated sugar
¾   cup packed brown sugar
    Dash salt
⅔   cup milk
¼   cup peanut butter
2   tablespoons butter

❶ Spray 13x9-inch pan with nonstick cooking spray. Place marshmallow fourths on bottom.

❷ In large saucepan, stir together granulated sugar, brown sugar, salt and milk; heat to 240°F (soft-ball stage).

❸ Remove from heat; beat in peanut butter and butter until creamy. Pour over marshmallows while still hot. Chill; cut when cold.

About 100 pieces.

MOLASSES TAFFY

JOANNE DAEDA
HERMANTOWN, MINNESOTA

Here's my grandmother's recipe from the 1930s. Kids love making this candy by themselves.

2   cups molasses
2   teaspoons cider vinegar
1½ tablespoons shortening
⅛   teaspoon salt
½   teaspoon baking soda

❶ In large saucepan, heat molasses and vinegar over medium-low heat, stirring constantly, until candy thermometer reaches 250°F (hard-ball stage) or until syrup becomes brittle when tested in cold water. Remove from heat; add shortening, salt and soda. Stir until mixture stops foaming.

❷ Pour mixture onto greased 15x10x1-inch pan. When cool enough to pull, remove from pan. Pull until light in color and firm. Roll into thin rope; cut into pieces. Wrap pieces in parchment paper.

About 4 dozen candies.

PEANUT BRITTLE

JUDY RICHMOND
GORHAM, MAINE

Mom and I always spent two days before Christmas making cookies and candy. This recipe was one of my favorites. It was put in a basket to be shared with friends and guests, but some pieces were put in a tin just for our family.

1½ cups raw peanuts, skins on
1   cup sugar
½   cup light corn syrup
⅛   teaspoon salt
1   teaspoon butter
1   teaspoon vanilla
1   teaspoon baking soda

❶ In 1½-quart microwave-safe casserole, stir together peanuts, sugar, corn syrup and salt. Microwave on High 8 minutes, stirring well after 4 minutes. Stir in butter and vanilla. Microwave an additional 2 minutes. Add baking soda; quickly stir until light and foamy. Immediately pour onto lightly greased baking sheet; spread out very thin. When cool, break into small pieces. Store in airtight container.

12 servings.

CARAMEL POPCORN

JOHN JONES
NAMPA, IDAHO

This recipe is so easy, you don't even need a candy thermometer. You can also double it!

2   cups packed brown sugar
½   cup light corn syrup
1   cup butter
½   teaspoon vanilla
½   teaspoon baking soda
1   cup Virginia nuts or nuts of choice (optional)
6   quarts popped corn

❶ Heat oven to 250°F. In large saucepan, combine brown sugar, corn syrup and butter. Bring to a boil; remove from heat. Add vanilla and baking soda; stir well. Stir in nuts, if using.

❷ In another large bowl, pour mixture over popcorn; mix well. Spread popcorn evenly on 15x10x1-inch baking pan or sturdy baking sheet. Bake 1 hour, stirring every 15 minutes. Cool; break into pieces.

6½ quarts.

CANDIED WALNUTS

JUDITH MCGEE
VOLCANO, CALIFORNIA

My husband's family has made this snack for the Christmas holidays since he was a child. This is a great gift in place of the cookies I used to make.

2   cups packed brown sugar
1   cup granulated sugar
½   cup water
1½ lb. walnut halves
1   teaspoon ground cinnamon
¼   teaspoon ground cloves
     Dash salt

❶ In large saucepan, heat brown sugar, granulated sugar and water over medium heat until syrup reaches 300°F (hard-crack stage). Add walnuts, cinnamon, cloves and salt. Continue cooking, stirring until syrup crystallizes. Spread mixture on baking sheet. When cool, break apart large pieces. Store in covered jar.

About 2 lb.

PENUCHE

ROSEANN ILSTRUP
LAKESIDE, CALIFORNIA

We've had this candy around at Christmas for as long as I can remember. The neighbor kids always came around, especially at Christmas, for Penuche.

3   cups packed brown sugar
1   cup milk
2   tablespoons light corn syrup
2   tablespoons butter
1   teaspoon vanilla
1   cup chopped nuts (walnuts or pecans are best)

❶ In large saucepan, combine brown sugar, milk and corn syrup. Cook over low heat, stirring constantly, to 240°F (soft-ball stage). Remove from heat; add butter but do not stir. Cool to lukewarm. Add vanilla; beat mixture until it loses its gloss or until small amount holds its shape when dropped from spoon. Add nuts. Pour mixture in buttered 8-inch square pan. Cool completely. Cut into 1-inch pieces.

64 candies.

PEAR MINCEMEAT

PEAR MINCEMEAT

SUZANNE BERGSTEN
EDMONTON, ALBERTA, CANADA

This recipe brings the joy and goodness of our pear trees to others throughout the year. It originated from my childhood in once-secluded Varennes, Quebec.

6   lb. pears
1   orange
1   lemon
2   lb. raisins
5   cups sugar
¼   cup butter
2   teaspoons ground ginger
2   teaspoons ground cinnamon
2   teaspoons ground nutmeg
2   teaspoons ground allspice
1   teaspoon ground cloves
¾   cup white vinegar
¾   cup apple juice

❶ Quarter and core pears. Squeeze orange and lemon for juice, removing seeds. Mince or chop pears, orange peel and lemon peel.

❷ In large saucepan, mix pears, orange and lemon juice, orange and lemon peels, raisins, sugar, butter, ginger, cinnamon, nutmeg, allspice, cloves, vinegar and apple juice; bring to a boil. Simmer until thick, about 1½ hours. Pack in sterilized jars. Seal by processing in boiling water bath 25 minutes.

6 to 7 pints.

CHOCOLATE CARAMELS

PATRICK EVANS
EUGENE, OREGON

This recipe is handed down from my grandmother. She made this just before Christmas and sent it in a package every year until she passed away. It is my favorite Christmas candy.

2   cups chopped black walnuts
2   cups granulated sugar
1   cup packed brown sugar
⅛   teaspoon salt
½   cup butter
3   (1-oz.) squares unsweetened chocolate, cut in small pieces
1   cup light corn syrup
1   cup cream
1   tablespoon vanilla

❶ Spread walnuts in generously buttered 8- or 9-inch square pan; set aside.

❷ In large saucepan, combine granulated and brown sugars, salt, butter, chocolate, corn syrup and cream. Boil until temperature reaches 248°F (firm-ball stage). Remove from heat; stir in vanilla until blended. Pour quickly over walnuts in pan. When cool, cut into squares.

64 caramels.

GLASS CANDY

MARY BLESSING
NORTH VERNON, INDIANA

My son's 7th grade class made this recipe for a class project. He brought the recipe home and we've enjoyed it at Christmas for the last few years.

2   cups sugar
½   cup light corn syrup
½   cup hot water
    Powdered sugar

❶ Butter heavy medium skillet. Place in freezer ½ to 1 hour before cooking syrup.

❷ In skillet, heat sugar, corn syrup and hot water until candy thermometer reaches 310°F. Stir well; pour into cold skillet. Return skillet to freezer 5 to 10 minutes or until cool enough to handle. Lift candy from skillet; place in pan filled with powered sugar. With scissors, cut candy into squares. Work quickly, as candy hardens rapidly.

1½ lb.

GARDEN RELISH

CHOCOLATE PRALINE TOPPING

ROGER HICKUM
PLYMOUTH, NEW HAMPSHIRE

My friends tell me they look forward to my ice cream socials just to have this topping.

1   cup whipping cream
⅔   cup packed brown sugar
⅔   cup butter
1   cup semisweet chocolate chips
1   cup chopped pecans
    Ice cream

❶ In large saucepan, bring cream, brown sugar and butter to a boil over medium heat. Stir constantly; reduce heat. Simmer 2 minutes; remove from heat. Stir in chocolate chips until melted; add pecans. Serve warm over ice cream.

3 cups.

GARDEN RELISH

LAURAL MINEARD
DUBLIN, OHIO

Every outdoor get-together has to have this!

½   head cauliflower, cut in florets, sliced
2   carrots, cut in 1½-inch strips
2   ribs celery, cut in 1-inch pieces
1   medium green bell pepper, cut into 2-inch strips
1   (4-oz.) jar pimientos, drained, cut into thin strips
1   (3-oz.) jar pimiento-stuffed green olives, drained
¾   cup wine vinegar
½   cup olive oil or vegetable oil
¼   cup water
2   tablespoons sugar
1   teaspoon salt
½   teaspoon dried oregano, crushed
¼   teaspoon freshly ground pepper

❶ In large saucepan, combine cauliflower, carrots, celery, bell pepper, pimientos, olives, vinegar, oil, water, sugar, salt, oregano and pepper. Bring to a boil over medium-high heat, stirring occasionally. Reduce heat; simmer covered 5 minutes. Cool. Cover; refrigerate at least 24 hours, stirring occasionally. Drain before serving.

5 cups.

SKILLET FUDGE SAUCE

ELSA ALTSHOOL
LAS CRUCES, NEW MEXICO

I've been making this marvelous fudge sauce for over 40 years.

1   (6-oz.) pkg. bittersweet chocolate
1   (12-oz.) can evaporated milk
2   cups sugar
2   teaspoons instant coffee granules
2   tablespoons rum
½   teaspoon vanilla

❶ In large saucepan, melt chocolate over low heat. Stir in evaporated milk. Add sugar, coffee, rum and vanilla. Increase heat to medium-high; cook until sauce has thickened. Spoon into large jar with lid. Refrigerate as long as you wish. To serve as hot fudge sauce, warm jar in pan of simmering water.

3 cups.

REFRIGERATOR PICKLES

CAROLYN LUMSDEN
DRESSER, WISCONSIN

This recipe was given to me by a friend many years ago. Every summer I make several batches. The last batch stays delicious in the refrigerator for three months, so you can enjoy these pickles long after a late summer harvest.

6   cups sliced cucumbers
1   cup sliced onion
1   cup sliced green bell pepper
¼   cup salt
    Ice cubes
2   cups sugar
¾   cup cider vinegar
¾   cup white vinegar
1   teaspoon celery seeds
½   teaspoon dill seeds

❶ In large bowl, combine cucumbers, onion, bell pepper and salt. Cover with ice cubes; refrigerate 3 to 4 hours.

❷ In large saucepan, combine sugar, cider and white vinegars, celery seed and dill seed. Bring to a boil, stirring occasionally. Let cool.

❸ Drain cucumbers; rinse lightly. Cover cucumbers with cooled syrup. Cover; refrigerate 3 to 4 days before using. These pickles keep 3 months refrigerated.

2 quarts.

CRANBERRY KNOCKOUT

WILLIE PEARSON
HILLSBORO, TENNESSEE

This recipe comes from a woman I knew in Nashville. My daughter makes it every Thanksgiving and Christmas.

1   lb. fresh cranberries
2   cups sugar
1   cup chopped pecans
3   tablespoons lemon juice
¼   teaspoon salt
1   (10-oz.) jar orange marmalade

❶ Heat oven to 325°F. In Dutch oven, stir together cranberries and sugar. Bake covered 1 hour; cool slightly. Stir in pecans, lemon juice, salt and marmalade; refrigerate.

About 3 cups.

CHOW CHOW (OLD-FASHIONED HOT DOG RELISH)

JENNENE LEA
SANTA CLARA, CALIFORNIA

This recipe has been in my family for at least five generations. I have been eating it for as long as I can remember. I give jars of it away, and recipients always ask for more.

1   medium cabbage, chopped
6   medium onions, chopped
6   green bell peppers, coarsely chopped
1   quart chopped green tomatoes
¼   cup pickling salt
6   cups cider vinegar or distilled vinegar
2   tablespoons prepared mustard
2½   cups sugar
2   tablespoons mustard seeds
1   tablespoon mixed pickling spices
1½   teaspoons ground turmeric
1   teaspoon ground ginger

❶ In large bowl, combine cabbage, onions, bell peppers, tomatoes and pickling salt. Cover; refrigerate overnight. Drain.

❷ In kettle, mix vinegar and mustard. Stir in sugar, mustard seeds, pickling spices, turmeric and ginger. Simmer 2 minutes. Add vegetables; simmer 10 minutes. Immediately ladle into hot sterilized jars, filling to ¼ inch of top. Adjust lids. Process in boiling water 5 minutes. (Start timing when water returns to a boil.) Remove jars; cool on wire racks. Check jars for airtight seal.

6 quarts.

TEXAS BARBECUE SAUCE

JUDY RICHMOND
GORHAM, MAINE

This was Grandma's secret sauce.

½   cup finely chopped onion
2   tablespoons packed brown sugar
1   teaspoon salt
1   teaspoon dry mustard
2   tablespoons Worcestershire sauce
½   cup ketchup
½   cup water
¼   cup wine vinegar

❶ In large saucepan, combine onion, brown sugar, salt, mustard, Worcestershire, ketchup, water and vinegar; simmer 15 minutes.

About 1½ cups.

RECIPE INDEX

GENERAL INDEX